Knowledge Shall Increase

George Harris

Knowledge Shall Increase

Copyright © 2015 by George Harris

Eleviv Publishing Group
Houston, TX 77082

All rights reserved. No part of this book may be reproduced or transmitted in any form or by any means without written permission of the author.

Scripture quotations marked "KJV" are taken from the Holy Bible, King James Version (Public Domain).

ISBN-13: 978-0692578797
ISBN-10: 069257879

Printed in the United States of America

DEDICATION

I dedicate this book first to the Father, Son and Holy Spirit, and secondly to my mother, Margaret Ann Harris Heard and my great-grandmother, Ora Bennett Lee Big-Momma. I also would like to say that this book would not be possible if were not for A sweet young lady by the name of Ms. Carol Dobbs. I thank you and the world thanks you!

Signed... ... ...*George Harris*... ... ...

Table of Contents

Time According to God versus
Time According to Man 1
The True First Ressurection 6
Does God know everything? 12
Life! Or is it? 45
Identifying the Heart 63
Once saved, always saved, yes or no? 81
The Role that Denomic Forces Play in Our Lives 102
The one thing Jesus knew that we do not 157
In a nut shell #one 173
In a nut shell #two 175
In a nut shell #three 177
Burying your Talent 180
Two Brothers & Profound Effect 189
What makes Patience so Valuable? 213
Daddy's Love 218
Voices in my head 224
From Earth to Heaven, How Far? 229
The Invisible Me 244
Passing the Test 251
Reality, Eternity & Illusion 266

Preface

This book is the actual fulfillment of the final prophecy of Daniel 12:4 in which, he prophesied that knowledge would increase during the time of the end. He was told then to seal the book until the time of the end.

The book was ordered to be unsealed in the final chapter of the Bible; Revelation 22:10 announcing the opening of the seal mentioned in Rev 5:2, Revelation 22:13 announcing that the first Light mentioned and the last person speaking in the Holy Bible is Jesus and Revelation 22:16 confirming that he is the Beginning Light/Bright Morning Star in Genesis 1:3. Because he was the first and only Light in the beginning with the Father before He and His Father made the sun, moon, and stars on the 4th day in verse 14.

I am a member of Garden Oaks Church of Christ. Under Pastor John Tillman Jr. 4926 N. Shepherd Dr. Houston TX 77018

Chapter 1

Time According to God versus Time According to Man

To man 24 hours is a day, but to God a day equals 1,000 years of man's time. In (2nd Peter 3:8) it states "But, beloved, be not ignorant of this one thing, that one day is with the Lord as a thousand years, and a thousand years as one day."

This means that what man calls a thousand years, God calls it one day. That is what God calls a day. Now let us look at what God calls (yesterday.)

When 24 hours have passed, man calls it yesterday. Psalms 90:4 states, "For a thousand years in thy sight are but as yesterday when it is past, and as a watch in the night." The key words in this verse are (when it is past.) What this is saying is that when a time period of what man calls 1,000 years have passed, God calls that same past 1,000 years period of time, (yesterday.) So now we know what God calls a day and what he calls yesterday.

If more proof is needed. In Genesis 1:5 it states "And God called the light Day, and the darkness he called Night. And the evening and the morning were the first day." Genesis 1:8 it says, "And God called the firmament Heaven. And the evening and the morning were the second day." In (Genesis 1:13) it states, "And the evening and the morning were the third day. "In (Genesis 1:19) it states, "And the evening and the morning were the fourth day."

Now the question is this, how did God do his work of creation on the first, second and third days, when in fact fact he did not create the time period known to mankind as a day, until the fourth day? Genesis 1:16 reads "And God made two great lights; the greater light to rule the day, and the lesser light to rule night: he made the stars also." This means that there was no sun or moon or stars, on the first, second and third days of God's creative work. According to our life on the earth by man's standard, it is impossible for a day to come and go unless the sun rises and sits in the sky for a period of time, then the moon and stars come out for a period of time until the sun begins to come up again!

Genesis 1:15 explains that these lights are specifically designed for the earth, or in other words for man, not for God. God can see in complete darkness better than man can see in complete light. (Genesis 1:15) "And let them be for lights in the firmament of the heaven to give light upon the earth: and it was so." The confusing part is this, when you compare (Genesis 1:3) to (Genesis 1:14) you will find that the writer in (Genesis 1:3) states "And God said, let there be light: and there was light." But in (Genesis1:14) it states, "And God said, let there be lights…………" The big difference is this, one verse says light, which is singular, meaning only one and the other verse says lights, which is plural, meaning more than one. There are two kinds of light; one is the light that we see by, such as that which keeps us from stumbling around in the dark. The other is the light we walk in as Christians. The light we walk in as Christians is Christ!

The first three words in the book of Genesis are "In the beginning" and the first three words in the book of Saint John are "In the beginning". Although the words "In the beginning" are written in the Bible these two times in reference to the beginning of creation, there is only one beginning, so they are both referring to the same event, thus also referring to the same single Light!

However, it is in the book of John that we get a better understanding of the light mentioned in (Genesis 1:3). We must understand that when it comes down to these two kinds of light, the most important one is the one that we as Christians must walk in, which is Christ. That is why God created it first. (John 1:1-9)

> 1 "In the beginning was the word, and the word was with God, and the word was God.
> 2 The same was in the beginning with God.
> 3 All things were made by him; and without him was not anything made that was made.
> 4 In him was life; and the life was the light of men.
> 5 And the light shineth in darkness; and the darkness comprehended it not.
> 6 There was a man sent from God, whose name was John.
> 7 The same came for a witness, to bear witness of the light that all men through him might believe.
> 8 He was not that light, but was sent to bear witness of that light.
> 9 That was the true light, which lighteth every man that cometh into the world."

So we can now see that the light mentioned in Genesis 1:3 is not a physical light such as the sun, but rather it is the spiritual light which is the Son! In Revelation 22:5 it states, "And there shall be no night there; and *they need no candle, neither light of the sun; for the Lord God giveth them light: and they shall reign forever and ever."*

With all this having been said, there is still a need for more proof. In the book of Genesis 2:16&17 it states, *"And the Lord God commanded the man, saying, of every tree of the garden thou mayest freely eat: But of the tree of the knowledge of good and evil, thou shalt not eat of it: for in the day that thou eatest thereof thou shalt surely die."* What these two verses mean is that according to God's time, in which a thousand years is the equivalent of one day; God is telling Adam that in the same day that he bites of that tree he will for sure die that day. One thing is for sure, God does not lie! Genesis 5:5 states, *"And all the days that Adam lived were nine hundred and thirty years and he died."*

In other words, if Adam would have lived a total of 1,000 years after the moment he bit of the fruit of the tree then he would have made the good Lord out of a lie; but he did not. He only lived 930 years all together, period. So God's word still stands; He died that same day: if he would have lived 70 more years he would have proven the Lord to be incorrect, which is impossible.

Chapter 2

The True First Resurrection

This chapter is about the real first resurrection, not the resurrection that most, if not all, of the world thinks or believes was the first resurrection!

Those of us in the land of the living today seem to think that what Jesus did on the cross was beneficial only to those of the New Testament. But nothing could be further from the truth. The beneficial effect of his resurrection goes back to before the Old Testament was written. Now even though it started before the foundation of the earth itself, I am going to start where it started on the earth- when Abraham sacrificed Isaac! When I say Abraham sacrificed Isaac, I'm saying in God's eye, Abraham did indeed sacrifice Isaac. But in man's eye, he almost sacrificed him. In other words, Abraham was guilty of intent. By today's law, it doesn't matter if you murder someone or intended to murder them, you are still guilty. Either guilty of murder or guilty of intent to commit murder. God's judgment is the same way. In (Hebrews 4:12) it states, "For the word of God is quick, and powerful, and sharper, than any two-edged sword, piercing even to the dividing asunder of soul and spirit, and of the joints and marrow, and is a discerner of the thoughts and the intents of the heart."

So when Abraham sacrificed Isaac, his only son of a miracle birth, God officially announced He would sacrifice his only Son also of a miracle birth.

Genesis 22:16&18 states, 16 "And said, By myself have I sworn, saith the lord, for because thou hast done this thing, and hast not withheld thy son, thine only son: 18 And in thy seed shall all the nations of the earth be blessed; because thou hast obeyed my voice."

From the time Abraham began his journey to sacrifice Isaac was not 72 hours. Instead, it was the remainder of the first day starting from whatever time they left that morning , the entire second day, and when they arrived on the third day. Genesis 22:4 states, "Then on the third day Abraham lifted up his eyes, and saw the place afar off." Jesus's journey was not 72 hours either. His was also the remainder of the day that they killed him, the entire second day, and he reappeared early on the beginning of the third day, not at the completion of the third day. Although in both cases, their journeys touched three separate days, neither was a total of three full days. I said all that because I hope it puts your mind in the proper place in time to better understand the justification for his commitment to those who had passed on first, and then to those who were still in the land of the living.

I would like to first say that there is more than one land of the living. In (Matthew 22: 31&32) Jesus is referring to this other land of the living: 31. "But as touching the resurrection of the dead, have ye not read that which was spoken unto you by God, saying, 32. I am the God of Abraham, and the God of Isaac, and the God of Jacob? God is not the God of the dead, but of the living."

This is the place where the first resurrection of Jesus Christ took place. But I will tell you a little bit more about why, before I tell you how. First, I want to correctly explain the cleansing power of the blood of Christ past, present and future. The blood of Christ washed away the sins of all believers who lived and died before he was born. This is the blood covering the PAST. The blood of Christ washed away all sins of the believers who lived during the time that he was alive. This is the blood of Christ covering what was then, the PRESENT. The blood of Christ washed, and is continuing to wash away all the sins of the believers who came after he died and rose, and ascended into heaven. This is the blood of Christ covering the FUTURE.

We are all covered by belief and repentance from sin. The past believers died believing that he would come. The then present believers simply believed their own eyes and ears. We are the future believers, and we believe that he has already come, and will come again. Before the cross, during the cross and after the cross. All are believers.

For many years scholars have been baffled by (Matthew 27:53). No one seems to know its meaning. Let us start with the verse itself. Matthew 27:53 states, "And came out of the graves (after his resurrection,) and went into the holy city and appeared unto many." After his resurrection means just that! When Jesus went into hell, he first entered into what is called the lowest hell. Psalm 86:13 states, "For great is thy mercy toward me: and thou hast delivered my soul from the lowest hell." This is the place where people go who have died in their sins as nonbelievers, a place of suffering.

We need to keep in mind that Jesus is not taking the place of a man who died a righteous death, but of a man who is a sinner, and so he died a sinner's death. This meant he had to receive a sinner's punishment. So the place he went to is the very definition of death. Here is a description of the place he went to. Luke16:23-26 states, 23 "And in hell he lift up his eyes," (notice that the rich man had to look up to see Lazarus in Abraham's bosom, meaning he was in a location lower than that of Lazarus and Abraham, yet all three were in hell.) "being in torments, and seeth Abraham afar off, and Lazarus in his bosom. 24 And he cried and said, Father Abraham, have mercy on me, and send Lazarus, that he may dip the tip of his finger in water, and cool my tongue; for I am tormented is this flame. 25 But Abraham said, Son, remember that thou in thy lifetime receivedst thy good things, and likewise Lazarus evil things: but now he is comforted, and thou art tormented. 26 And beside all this, between us and you there is a GREAT GULF fixed: so that they which would pass from hence to you cannot; neither can they pass to us that would come from thence."

Now I want to draw your attention to the part about the great gulf. The place where the rich man was is where Jesus went to first. The place where Abraham was is the place where Jesus went to second. No one has ever risen from where Jesus was at first, which is the fire and crossed the GREAT GULF, and entered into the location in hell that is called paradise. To do so is the first definition of the word RESURRECTION!

The second definition of resurrection is when he returned to the world we now live in, back into his flesh. It is not possible to pay the price for one sinner, let alone the world, unless you pay the full price for a man who dies in his sins. The full price for dying in my sins, as a none-believer, would be to first die from off the face of the earth. Then go to where the fire and pain and suffering is in hell. Now to rise from that place is the textbook definition of the word RESURRECTION! And the souls in paradise witnessed it first.

Remember, Jesus told the man on the cross beside him that he would be with him that same day in paradise, the place in hell where there is no pain and no suffering. Luke23:43 states, "And Jesus said unto him, Verily I say unto thee, today shall thou be with me in paradise."

Chapter 3

Does God Know Everything?

Well I guess I will have to start from the beginning with this particular revelation. It started when I was in Cleveland, Ohio. I was in a religious program there, and one day the program director of gathered us all together to give a class on the subject of predestination. (The word predestinate means to predetermine the outcome of a thing or situation before it even begins.)

As the director, whom I am pretty sure was an ordained minister, began teaching on this subject, I, in my spirit, began to sense that he was trying to indicate something, without actually saying it. So I began asking him questions that were designed to push or coerce him into saying exactly what he meant when he said, "God knows everything."

As it turns out, he answered all of my questions, but his answers were what I would call semi-evasive. So I decided to ask him flat out, "Are you saying God knows before we are born, when we are going to die, everything we are going to do in our lifetime, and whether we are going to heaven or to the lake of fire when we die?" All this before we are even born? His answer to the question was, "Yes, that is exactly what I am saying." And I believe my immediate response was, "Sir you are incorrect!" And I went on to say, not necessarily in this order, that scripture states that Jesus said, "My sheep know my voice", and Sir, I do not recognize your voice.

John 10:4&5 states, 4"And he putteth forth his own sheep he goeth before them, and the sheep follow him: for they know his voice. 5 And a stranger they will not follow, but will flee from him: for they know not the voice of a stranger."

I told the director; first of all, what you are saying is not the Gospel. The word Gospel means good news, and what you are saying is not good news. Anyone who believes what you are saying, along with their own ability to rationalize, would soon come to the conclusion that, if God already knows whether or not they are going to make it to heaven, before they are even born, then it doesn't matter at all how they live their lives, or whether they obey or disobey the Lord. Because the decision has already been made by God himself, and no one can change the mind of God! This belief alone would cause people to give up hope instead of hanging on to the *hope that they might make it. The only thing a person could hope for is that the Lord has already decided to allow them to enter the kingdom of Heaven before they were even born! If this line of teaching is correct, then Faith is useless. The scripture states (Hebrews 11:1) "Now faith is the substance of things hoped for, the evidence of things not seen."*

At this point the Lord led me to some scriptures in the Old Testament that exemplify the word predestinate, perfectly. Before I get into these scriptures, I remind you again that the word predestinate, means to predetermine the end of a matter, before it even begins! In Deuteronomy 28:1-14, the Lord, by the mouth of Moses, tells the children of Israel, all the things that he himself has already predestinated them to, from the very beginning to the very end, exactly how it will take place (IF) they walk the righteous path of obedience! I emphasize the word path because a path is something that we, the children of God, are always on. We begin life on what is called a path. When our life ends, it will end on a path. All paths lead to one of two final destinations, to either heaven or to the lake of fire! In other words, he is telling the end before it even begins.

Deuteronomy 28:1-14 states, 1 "And it shall come to pass, if thou shalt hearken diligently unto the voice of the Lord thy God, to observe and to do all his com-

mandments which I command thee this day, that the Lord thy God will set thee on high above all nations of the earth: 2 And all these blessing shall come on thee, and overtake thee, if thou shalt hearken unto the voice of the Lord thy God. 3 Blessed shalt thou be in the city, and blessed shalt thou be blessed in the field. 4 Blessed shall be the fruit of thy body, and the fruit of thy ground, and the fruit of thy cattle, the increase of thy kin, and the flocks of thy sheep. 5 Blessed shall be thy basket and thy store. 6 Blessed shalt thy be when thou comest in, and blessed shalt thou be when thou goest out."

It goes on to say, " 7 The Lord shall cause thine enemies that rise up against thee to be smitten before thy face: they shall come out against thee one way, and flee before thee seven ways. 8 The Lord shall command the blessing upon thee in thy storehouses, and in all thou settest thine hand unto; and he shall bless thee in the land which the lord thy God giveth thee. 9 The Lord shall establish thee an holy people unto himself, as he hath sworn unto thee, if thou shalt keep the commandments of the Lord thy God, and walk in his ways. 10 And all people of the earth shall see that thou art called by the name of the Lord, and they shall be afraid of thee. 11 And the Lord shall make thee plenteous in goods, in the fruit of thy body, and in the fruit of thy cattle, and in the fruit of thy ground, and in the land *which the Lord sware unto thy fathers to give thee. 12 The Lord shall open unto thee his good treasure, the heaven to give rain unto thy land in his season, and to bless all the work of thine hand: and thou shalt lend unto many nations, and thou shalt not borrow. 13 And the Lord shall make thee the head, and not the tail; and thou shalt be above only, and thou shalt not be beneath; if that thou hearken unto the commandments of the Lord thy God, which I command thee this day, to observe and to do them: 14 And thou shalt not go aside from any of the words which I command thee this day, to the right hand, or to the left to go after other gods to serve them."*

In the 14 scriptures I just quoted, the Lord told the children of Israel about one of the two paths that he has laid out for them before they were ever born! And in the next few passages of scripture that I am going to quote, he is going to tell them about the other path that he has laid out for them, and this path was also laid out for them before they were born!

In (Deuteronomy 28:15-29+48) the scripture states, 15 "But it shall come to pass, if thou will not hearken unto the voice of the Lord thy God, to observe to do all his commandments and his statutes which I command thee this day; that all these curses shall come upon thee, and overtake thee: 16 Cursed shalt thou be in the city, and cursed shalt thou be in the field. 17 Cursed shall be thou basket and thy store. 18 Cursed shall be the fruit of thy body, and the fruit of thy land, the increase of thy kine, and the flocks of thy sheep. 19 Cursed shalt thou be when thou comest in, and cursed shalt thou be when thou goest out. 20. The Lord shall send upon thee cursings, vexation, and rebuke, in all that thou settest thine hand unto for to do, until thou be destroyed, and until thou perish quickly; because of the wickedness of thy doings, whereby thou hast forsaken me."

The scripture goes on to say, 21 "The Lord shall make the pestilence cleave unto thee, until he have consumed thee from off the land, whither thou goest to possess it. 22 The Lord shall smite the with a consumption, and with a fever, and with an inflammation, and with an extreme burning, and with the sword, and with blasting, and with mildew; and they shall pursue thee until thou perish. 23 And thy heaven that is over thy head shall be brass, and the earth that is under thee shall be iron. 24 The Lord shall make the rain of thy land powder and dust: from heaven shall it come down upon the, until thou be destroyed. 25 The Lord shall cause thee to be smitten before thine enemies: thou shalt go out one way against them, and flee seven ways before them: and shalt be removed into all the kingdoms of the earth. 26 And thy carcass shall be meat unto all fowls of the air, *and unto the beast of the earth, and no man shall fray them away. 27 The Lord will smite thee with the botch of Egypt, and with the emerods, and with the scab, and with the itch, whereof thou canst not be healed. 28 The Lord shall smite thee with madness, and blindness, and astonishment of heart: 29 And thou shalt grope at noonday, as the blind gropeth in darkness, and thou shalt not prosper in thy ways: and thou shalt be only oppressed and spoiled evermore, and no man shall save thee."* +48. *"Therefore shalt thou serve thine enemies which the Lord shall send against thee, in hunger, and in thirst, and in nakedness, and in want of all things: and he shall put a yoke of iron upon thy neck, until he has destroyed thee."*

Now the thing to remember is that God laid out both paths before they were even born, and after they were born they themselves chose what path they would walk in! In the book of (Deuteronomy 30:19) it states, 19. "I call heaven and earth to record this day against you, that I have set before you life and death, blessing and cursing: therefore choose life that both thou and thy seed shall live:"

In order for the word of God to be useful to those who read it, the Reader must first understand what he or she has read. There is a simple version of the understanding of the verses you have just now read. The simple conclusion is this, every human being who enters into this world has, (for the sake of simplicity), already been predestinated to, not just one destiny, but a minimum of two. That's right, a minimum of two. In other words, before you were even born, the Lord God all mighty laid a minimum of two paths for you to walk in during your lifetime, one positive and the other negative.

Let me first say this; when we hear the word prophecy in the Bible, we always think there is only one way the situation can possibly turn out. But even in the case of prophecy, there is always more than one way for the situation to turn out– a positive and a negative. There was prophecy concerning Judas Iscariot, which for him was negative, but for the world it was positive. What many of us today do not know is that it was possible at the time for Judas to turn down the 30 pieces of silver, and possible for him to refuse to betray Jesus. Just because God himself reveals to his prophet, a positive prophecy concerning a particular individual, that does not mean there is no negative prophecy in existence concerning that same individual. It is very likely that the entire world believes it was impossible for Jesus to do anything other than the things that were prophesied of him, concerning the things he would do while he was on the earth. But the truth is that it was possible for even Jesus himself to deviate from God's original plan.

The reason I am sure that the Lord has directed me to say this is because, number one, Jesus never told a lie, and number two, the scripture does not lie, and scripture says Jesus said that it was possible for him to call the whole thing off and all he had to do was say the words, and his Father in heaven would stop everything and send angels to rescue him! What many of us fail to understand is that Jesus was not, and is not, some kind of robot programmed to obey his Father. He was and still is a Son who was taught to do the right thing by his Father. Many of us were taught to do the right thing by the same Father, yet we do the wrong thing!

In the next four scriptures I quote, you will see for yourself that Jesus is saying to one of the disciples fighting to save him, that he can call on the Father to rescue him if he decided to; in other words, he can deviate from his Father's plan if he decides to do so!

Pay close attention to verse #53. Matthew 26:51-54 states: 51 "And, behold, one of them which were with Jesus stretched out his hand, and drew his sword, and struck a servant of the high priest's, and smote off his ear. 52 Then said Jesus unto him, Put up again thy sword unto his place: for all they that take the sword shall perish with the sword. 53 Thinkest thou that I cannot now pray to my Father, and he shall presently give me more than twelve legions of angels? 54 But how then shall the scriptures be fulfilled, that thus it must be?"

So he did have the option to divert from all that was prophesied about him! When we read scriptures such as Romans 8:29&30, we must also take into consideration the fact that in the Lord's foreknowledge of us, and he foreknew all of us before we were even conceived; in his foreknowledge of each of us, he saw beforehand, both the negative and the positive outcomes of our lives, and he went ahead and blessed, ordained and sanctified our positive outcome; and likewise concerning our negative outcome, he went ahead and cursed it and condemned it. However, many times in the scripture, it only speaks about the positive outcome.

I am just a man like any other man, but have been prophesied over concerning the work the Lord has called me and prepared me to do. But for some reason, there was something in me that halfway led me to believe that even though I was walking in sin, there was no way I could die in my sin before I do the things prophesied for me to do. I knew that after I accomplished His will for my life, if I turn back to a life of sin, I could die in my sins. But for some reason I halfway thought it could not happen before I had done his will. But one night I had a vision, and in that vision the Lord made it crystal clear to me that I was wrong, and that I stood a very good chance of dying in my sin before I accomplished the things he has predestinated me to do!

Romans 8:29&30 states, 29 "For whom he did foreknow, he also did predestinate to be conformed to the image of his son, that he might be the firstborn among many brethren. 30 Moreover whom he did predestinate, them he also called: and whom he called, them he also justified: and whom he justified, them he also glorified."

Now we are going to get into a more complicated version of the things the Lord has shown to me. But before that, I want to take a little time to make sure you and I are on the same page concerning the question, Does God know everything? First, we have to get a proper understanding of the word "everything."

No matter how long a man lives on earth, there are only two things he can do, obey the Lord or disobey the Lord! There is no third option. God knows everything that will happen in a man's life if the man obeys him. This is one half! God also knows everything that will happen in a man's life if the man disobeys him. This is the other half! When the Lord puts the two halves together, he then knows Every-Thing! All of this takes place before he places us in our mother's womb, and then we are born, at which point, he begins to do, not everything within his power, but everything he will allow himself to do, in order to persuade us to walk in the Path that leads to heaven!

As I said before, this is the simple version. Now comes the more complicated version. After I received the exact scriptures from the Lord, and the correct understanding, the class was over and I began writing down what the Lord had just finished giving me. I didn't want to somehow lose or forget any of this particular revelation. Because it was my first time hearing it, even though I was the one saying it in the class. The people in the class with me probably thought I already knew it, but the truth is I didn't. That is one of the many things about the Lord that never ceases to amaze me; how he can put his words in a man's mouth in such a way that it seems like it came out of that man's own mind.

Now, although it was under different circumstances, I am still reminded of Luke 12:11&12 where it states, 11 "And when they bring you unto the synagogues, and unto magistrates, and powers, take ye no thought how or what thing ye shall answer, or what ye shall say: 12 For the Holy Ghost shall teach you in the same hour what ye ought to say."

While I was in the process of writing down the first revelation, the Lord hit me with what I would call the second part of that same revelation. For lack of words, I guess I would say that in my spirit, the Lord caused me to know exactly how he does it. What I mean is, the Lord showed me exactly how he knows what we are going to do before we do it, and it was so instant that I had to get up out of my chair and run outside to get some fresh air. After I was outside for a little while, and had calmed myself down a little bit, I asked the Lord in so many words, more or less; and I'll never forget this. I said, "Lord: How in the world will I be able to cause the world to believe what you have just shown me?" And instantly he placed one word in my heart, soul, sprit and mind, and that one word was the word DEJAVU!

I suppose I need to go ahead and share what was shown to me. But before I start, I just want to say that when I witnessed the magnitude of his love, care, concern, commitment and meticulousness of his work on us, and total devotion to us, before he ever placed us in our mother's womb, I was completely devastated!

This is what was shown to me. Jeremiah 1:5 states, "Before I formed thee in the belly I knew thee; and before thou camest forth out of the womb I sanctified thee, and I ordained thee a prophet unto the nations." Before you were placed inside your mother's body, the lord created all of your paths that you will travel in for your entire lifetime. When I said all, I mean All. What I mean by all, is this; there are many paths that lead to destruction, and there are many paths that lead to eternal life. There are paths that lead to you being physically injured. There are paths that lead to you escaping injury. *Some paths lead you to death at age 27. Other paths lead you to death at the ripe old age of 95. There are paths that lead you to becoming pregnant, and others that lead to not becoming pregnant. There are paths that lead you to killing someone or not killing anyone. A path may lead you to becoming the president of the United States of America. A path may lead you to not becoming the president of the United States of America. There are paths that lead you to becoming addicted to crack cocaine, and paths that lead you to not becoming addicted. There are paths that lead you to remaining addicted to drugs. There are paths that lead you to getting off drugs. There are paths that lead you to becoming rich and famous, as well as those that lead you to being poor and unknown. If there is a path that leads you to homosexuality, then there is a path that leads you away from it.*

It would take me a lifetime if I tried to list all the paths that the Lord has created for each of us. Before you were conceived, the Lord created all these paths, and many, many, many more. Then he took you, (now keep in mind, the fact that you have not yet been even so much as conceived), then the Lord took you, and placed you on your own individual path's beginning, which branches off to thousands, if not millions of other paths and directions. Then he takes you down, not just some of them or most of them, but all of them in order to see what you will do, what you will say, how you will react in every situation, and what the outcome will be. He took you to every crossroad and took you to the left and to the right. He took you straight ahead, and he also took you backwards. He put you through every possible scenario. You can walk half way down a road or path and change your mind and turn back, or go one fourth of the way, and change your mind, it does not matter. He took you down every path, both good and bad, and he saw exactly how every path ended.

I hope what I am about to say does not confuse you, but every event on your individual path in this world is waiting for you to either chose it or pass it by. Now if the event itself is waiting on you, then that proves that the event was here before you got here. We do not make our own destiny, we chose our own destiny!

Ecclesiastes 1:9&10 states, 9 "The thing that have been, it is that which shall be; and that which is done is that which shall be done: and there is no new thing under the sun. 10 Is there anything whereof it may be said, See, this is new? It hath been already of old time, which was before us."

In your lifetime while here on earth you will not travel all the way to the end of all the paths the Lord laid out for you, because many of the paths that you start to go down, you do not go all the way to the end of and many of them you never even start.

You went all the way down these Paths when you were still just a spirit, and had not yet been placed inside the flesh you now live in. Right now a man might say, "I am only flesh and bone," but you could not say that back then, because at that time you had not yet received either flesh nor bone. But now that you have been born, and are living inside the body, you may, for example, go halfway, and change your mind and turn off that path, or maybe even go back to the point where you got on that path, and take another path. Remember this, the Lord and his angels are working with you at all times to try to lead you in the right direction. They do this in a number of different ways.

Let's say, for example, you are walking down a path that leads to both physical and spiritual death, and you are unaware of it. But the Lord is aware of it because he has already taken you to the end of that path when you were still just a spirit without flesh. So he might send another Christian to warn you about the path you are traveling. He may give a mother a uncomfortable feeling about her son or daughter, and the mother tells the child to stay at home that night, instead of going out to the nightclub. The child stays at home while there *friends go out and get killed or hurt in a car accident on their way back home from the club.*

The person on the path that ends in death may go to church and the preacher, having received a message from the Lord, changes his mind about the sermon he had intended to preach, and instead preaches a message on the very subject the Lord wants the person on the path to death to hear. And as a result, that person gets off that path, escapes death, and never knows how close he or she has come to death!

Sometimes when we are on a path that is about to end in death, the Lord will wait until we go to sleep and come to us in a dream, or in what we call a nightmare, to warn us something bad is about to happen to us, if we don't get on anther path. It may not be a warning against something we are doing. It may be a warning against something we have made up our minds to do. Job 33:14-18 states, 14 "For God speaketh once, yea twice, yet man perceiveth it not. 15. In a dream, in a vision of the night, when deep sleep falleth upon men, in slumbering upon the bed: 16. Then he openeth the ears of men, and sealeth their instruction, 17. That he may withdraw man from his purpose, and hide pride from man. 18. He keepeth back his soul from the pit, and his life from perishing by the sword." (The word pit means grave.)

There are things we are going to do, that we have no idea we are going to do. But the Lord knows, because of the path we are on. Remember, he knows everything that is going to take place on whatever path we are on. He also knows about the things that we plan to do, because he listened as we talked over the plan with ourselves, within our own mind.

Not only that, he is involved with the conversation we have within ourselves. He is that still, quiet voice whispering in our ear, telling us not to do whatever wrong thing we are about to do. So if he is not able to persuade us to change our minds with his quiet still voice, which we call our continence, how can he not know beforehand, exactly what it is that we plan to do? Now I did say plan to do, not going to do, because what we plan to do and what we actually do is not always the same. The mere fact his voice tries to persuade us to go the other way proves that he is present during the time we are discussing the matter internally. He is always a step or two ahead of us.

I am not one to give our adversary any credit, or praise, so don't think that I am praising the enemy when I say that due to the fact the devil is also present when we are having that conversation in our mind, as to whether or not to do the right thing or the wrong thing, he also remains a step or two ahead of us. If he convinc-

es us to do the wrong thing, then he will prepare a trap for us, and if he cannot persuade us with his not-so small, and not-so still voice, then he starts working on another way to persuade us.

Those of us who study the Bible on a regular basis might ask, "If it is true that the Lord does not know before we are born whether or not we are going to go to heaven or to the lake of fire, when we die, then what about Pharaoh?" The answer to that question is this: If a child is raised by his parents to do the wrong thing, and that child does indeed do the wrong thing, then who is responsible for the child doing the wrong thing, the child or its parents? The obvious answer is the child's parents are responsible. Because if he does the right thing, instead of the wrong thing, then the child would have to be considered a disobedient child as far as his parents are concerned. God himself raised up Pharaoh to do what looks like to us the wrong thing, but what Pharaoh actually did was he obeyed the voice of his parent, God. So the responsibility lies on God! The scripture does not say that Pharaoh was condemned for what he did. Obeying the Lord does not condemn a man. Disobeying the lord is what condemns a man. Pharaoh died obeying the Lord.

Exodus 9:16 states, "And in very deed for this cause have I raised thee up, for to shew in thee my power; and that my name might be declared throughout all the earth." Any man attempting to compare himself and his circumstances with Pharaoh and his circumstances, that that man is in error. Because in 2nd Corinthians 10:12 it states, "For we dare not make ourselves of the number, or compare ourselves with some that commend themselves: but they measuring themselves by themselves, and comparing themselves among themselves, are not wise." Never before in the history of the world, has the Lord ever commanded a human being to commit a sin! The Lord told a prophet to marry a prostitute, which was a violation of the law. (Hosea 1:2) Had the prophet disobeyed God and obeyed the law, then he would have sinned. Because it is a sin to disobey God.

There is another scripture many so-called Bible scholars and theologians will use to try to prove the Lord knows before we are born whether we are going to heaven when we die or to the lake of fire. That would be the scriptures and prophecies concerning Judas Iscariot, who betrayed Jesus. The reason they use Judas to try to prove their point is because the prophecy concerning Judas does indeed seem to indicate that he was condemned before he was even born. But if we look into the prophecy itself we will find that in (Acts 1: 20) there is no mentioning of Judas's condemnation; it does ask that his bishoprick be replaced. The word bishoprick means "position as a bishop." In (Acts 1:20) it states,

"For it is written in the book of Psalms, Let his habitation be desolate and let no man dwell therein: and his bishoprick let another take."

Now in (Psalms 69:25-28), the writer David is asking that they not be forgiven because of what they did to Jesus. These are the words of David which included prophecy, but also David's own desire that this person be condemned, especially in verse# 28 where David prayed that their name be erased out of the book of life. But none of those things did Jesus desires for Judas, because Jesus forgave Judas for what he had done! Now ironically enough, Jesus was the only one to let it be known that the man who betrayed him would be condemned. But not because of what he did to Jesus. Judas was on a path, and Jesus could see what that path lead to; Jesus did not see Judas being condemned for betraying him, because he himself forgave him of that particular sin, and when Jesus forgives you for a sin, then that sin definitely cannot condemn you.

Earlier in this book I explained how repentance must come before forgiveness of sin can take place. Judas did indeed repent of the sin of betraying Jesus. Matthew 27:3-5 states, 3 *"Then Judas, which had betrayed him, when he saw that he was condemned,"* (At this point Judas realizes that although he did not know what to expect, one thing was for sure, this was not what he expected.) "repented himself, and brought again the thirty pieces of silver to the chief priests and elders, 4. Saying, I have sinned in that I have betrayed the innocent blood. And they said, What is that to us? see thou to that. 5. And he cast down the pieces of silver in the temple, and departed," (At this point Judas was safe, and had not yet entered a state of condemnation.) "and went and hanged himself." However, it is at this point that Judas entered into condemnation, closed the door, and threw away the key.

Jesus is the one who taught the world that we must forgive each other no matter what they do to you, even if they betrayed you, and caused you to lose your life. So we know for sure Jesus forgave him. The thing that Jesus saw that would condemn Judas was what Judas would do next and what Judas did next was commit suicide! Jesus simply looked at the negative path Judas was on, but don't forget that Judas also had a positive path as well. All of us do!

Matthew 26:24 states, "The Son of man goeth as it is written of him: but woe unto that man by whom the Son of man is betrayed! It had been good for that man if he had not been born." As I said before, Jesus was prophesied about more than any man in the history of the world. The prophesy was that he would be condemned to being crucified, which is a positive outcome for both

Jesus as well as the whole world. The average person would look at the facts given, pertaining to Jesus' life, and somehow arrive at the conclusion that Jesus was condemned to be crucified before he was ever even born! And that there was no way he could do anything, other than that which was prophesied, that he would do. Well that sounds correct, and I myself am tempted to agree with the average man who arrived at that conclusion. But if I were to do so, then I would be just as incorrect as the average man. Why? Because lo and behold, Jesus himself said that he did not have to volunteer to do the things that where prophesized about him; and that he could call the whole thing off if he decided to. Which would be a negative outcome! He even said in a conversation once that if he did not go through with it, then how will the prophecy be fulfilled. Matthew 26:54 states, "But how then shall the scriptures be fulfilled, that thus it must be?" So you see Jesus had a choice.

If Jesus and Judas where both locked in the same prophesy, and we now see that Jesus in fact, did have a choice in the matter, then how can anyone say that Judas did not.!? God himself, said that what Pharaoh did was not his fault, but he said no such thing concerning Judas. So the answer to the question; Was Judas condemned before he was ever even born? The answer is no. Judas was not condemned to die and burn in the lake of fire before he was even born.

As I started to mention before, after I received this revelation, I ran outside because I was overwhelmed. After I caught my breath and calmed down, I asked the Lord a question, and that question was, "How in the world will I be able to convince the world that this revelation came from you?" And it was right then and there that the spirit of the Lord spoke to me, and said only one word. That word was DEJAVU! After he said the word dejavu, he then began to explain to me what dejavu really is. Before I explain what was shown to me, I will give you the dictionary definition of the word. (Dejavu is a French word which literally means "already seen," the phenomenon of remembering an event currently being experienced, even though it is the first time in the person's life that he or she has ever experienced the event.)

In order to paint a clearer picture, let us just say, for example, a man takes a trip to New York City for the first time in his life, and he is having dinner at a restaurant. The waitress at the table directly in front of him falls to the floor and begins to go into an epileptic seizure. The man jumps up from his seat and rushes to her aid. He turns her over on her side, holds her head in his lap and asks someone for a cold, wet towel. Another *waitress runs over and hands him the towel. He wipes the woman's face over and over, while whispering words of comfort in her ear until the paramedics arrive to take the waitress away in the ambulance. After the incident is over, the man tells his friend, who was with him at the time, that he remembers the entire scene. He remembers being there before and doing what he'd done. He remembers doing it all before. He's not saying that he remembers it in a dream, he is saying that he literally remembers doing it before!*

He is confused because in his mind, he is asking himself, "How can I remember seeing and doing all of this, if I have never, ever done anything like this in my entire life? And this is the first time I've ever been to New York City in my life!" As long as he has been living in the flesh, he has never before in his life, been to New York City. So his question to himself is why does he feel like this is his second time doing this when he knows for a fact that this is the first time this has ever happened.

What the spirit revealed to me was this; the reason why the man feels as though this is his second time seeing and experiencing this particular scene is because, actually, this was his second time seeing and experiencing this event. The first time that he saw and experienced this event was before he was born!

As I stated earlier, before we are born, before we are even conceived in our mother's womb, the Lord created for each of us our own individual path, with both positive and negative consequences. So for the sake of simplicity, we will call this path the Master Path. On the master path there is a path of obedience containing positive consequences, as well as a path of disobedience, containing negative consequences. Remember, even though we have both negative and positive paths within our own individual path, it is still only one overall path that we are on, called the master path.

I also said earlier that after He created our individual paths, He then placed us on our own individual path, and then took us to the end of every path within our path in order to know how every path must end, which includes every possible scenario.

Now listen very carefully to what I am about to say! It was during this time; in other words, while the Lord was in the process of carrying or leading us down every path; that we had our spirit-eyes and spirit ears open throughout the entire process, from beginning to end. In fact, all of our senses that we have now, we had then. I say this because there are some who were born blind or deaf, and if a person is blind or deaf now, then they were blind or deaf then also. The understanding that I am trying to convey is this; as the Lord took us through this process in order to witness every possibility of the life that we were about to live, we also witnessed it at that same time. Because you have witnessed all of the scenes in your life before you were born, this means that you have within you the capacity to recognize or remember any given scene when you see, or experience it again. Now what you and I do not have is the capacity to select which scenes we wish to remember. The Lord God Almighty is the only one with the capacity to select the scenes he will allow us to recognize or remember.

The Lord, at this time, has not revealed to me all of his reasons for allowing us to experience what we call Dejavu. But he has revealed to me that one of his Reasons for allowing us to experience Dejavu, is because it serves as proof that whatever we do for the first time on the earth while living in the flesh, is not the first time. The first time was in heaven, before we were born, and the second time is on earth after we were born. So we now know what the scriptures mean by the statement "There is nothing new under the sun." Ecclesiastes 1:9 states, "The thing that hath been, it is that which shall be; and that which is done is that which shall be done: and there is no new thing under the sun." The things that I have done as a spirit, having not yet received my body of flesh, is that which I shall do when I do receive my fleshly body, and that which I have done up there is that which shall be done by me down here. So nothing is new down here under the sun!

That is not all that the Lord revealed to me on this particular subject; there is more. But before I go into that part, I want to say this; the Lord did not give me all of this revelation at one time. It seems to me, as though he gave me different revelations at different locations. I don't know why he did it that way. But I think it was because I most likely would not have been able to handle it all at one time. I think that this last part was due to the fact that after I had time to absorb all of the things he had at that point revealed to me, there was a question that popped up in my mind. Now to be perfectly honest, I do not know whether it was my own natural curiosity that caused me to ask this question or whether the Lord simply caused my mind to ask this question. But I am more inclined to believe that it was the Lord's doing.

The question came to me like this: There are billions of people living on the earth at any given time period and we are all traveling on different paths at the same time, so there is no doubt as to whether or not we cross one another's paths because we do. Everything I do on my path affects someone else on their path. For example, if I, while on my path in life, decide to go to the store at 9:45 pm because the store closes at 10:00 pm, *and it takes me 5 minutes to get to the store, so I arrive at the store at 9:50 pm. But let us just say that on that same night the store manager, while on his path in life, decides to change his mind about closing the store at 10:00 pm and instead closes at 9:30 pm. And as a result, I end up having to wait until in the morning to get what I want from that store. Now you can clearly see how the store manager's path affected my path. You see if the store manager would have decided differently while on his path in life, then my path would have turned out differently.*

So the question that came up was: How is it possible that you, Lord, are able to take over a billion people, having over a billion individual different paths, with all of them changing the directions that they travel on their own individual paths whenever they decide to do so; aside from the fact that when they do so they change or affect the path of any given number of people living in the world at the same time that they themselves are living; not to mention the affect they have on the unborn?

The answer I received to that question gave me an immeasurable amount of reverence to the sheer intelligence of the mind of God! I mean that if you totally set aside all of God's ability to perform miracles and just focus on his mental capacity, you would soon realize how dangerous a person would be if they had only one one-hundredth of one percent of God's mental capacity. It also gives new meaning to the word multitasking!

The answer revealed to me was this, in order for the Lord to accurately know the outcome of each person in the world, based upon the path they are on, including each one's prerogative to change directions at any given moment. And also including the changing effects the paths have on each other. The Lord took me, for example, and set me on my own path and, (for the sake of making this easier to comprehend, I will only use a small number like 10 other people, besides myself). He took me and set me on my path, and he then took 10 other people and put them on their own paths, and then caused each of them and their path to cross me and my path. Then he caused me and each one of the other 10 people, one at a time, to go through every possible scenario concerning each of their actions, and what my response would be to each of their individual actions.

Then he ran them through every possible scenario concerning my actions in order to know their response to my actions. Now all of this was done first involving only two people. This entire process has to be repeated nine more times because there are nine more individuals included in this example, 11 of us all together.

But it does not end there because when I am removed from the equation there remains 10 and one of the 10 has to be put through the process with the other nine and that would leave nine, and then one of the nine would have to be processed with the remaining eight, and so on and so on. In reality, we are looking at much larger numbers, as well as much more than one individual added to the equation at a time. So I only used 11 people to illustrate what all took place before we were even born. I don't know about anyone else, but I myself consider the processing of these 11 to be meticulously complicated. Not to mention the fact that he can have an on-going conversation with every human being on the earth at the same time in God only knows how many different languages. HE REALLY IS GOD!

I had intended to stop at this point, but the Holy Spirit moved me to give yet another, simpler example. I do not know all of the reasons why, but it must be very important to the Lord that you understand this part of this book. So here is the other example, which is almost exactly like the first example, except I will use only two people. Let us say there are only two people in the world; A man and a woman. Before the man and woman were born, the Lord first created a path for one of them, and a path for the other.

Then the Lord took both of them and put them on their own individual master path. Then he took one of them down their own individual path, to see what they would do in every situation their path presented. Then he took the other one down their own individual path, to see what they would do in every situation that their path presented to them. Then he took the one path, with one person on it, and crossed it with the other path with the other person on it.

Then he caused the one to do everything that they could possibly do, every word said, every thought toward the fact that this other person is also in the world that they live in, every scenario, starting from the day or night that the one met the other. Then he did the same thing with the other. When he was finished, he knew how every path in these two persons' lives would end. But he does not know what paths they will chose or whether they will stay on a path should they chose one, or will he have to try to persuade either or both of them to stay on the path they may choose or persuade them to get off immediately, because he does know how every path ends. But when they meet, and how they meet, will be determined by what each one of them do on their own individual paths. One may walk in a particular direction one day, while the other walks in a different direction on that same day. As a result, the two of them do not meet each other on that day! But let's just say that two days later they both happen to walk in the same direction and BOOM, they meet.

To us it seems as though every thought we think and every course of action that we take is original. But it is not. They all originated with God, it is just that there are so many options that we cannot help but feel and think as though we are in total control, when the true reality of it all is, we have the totality of limited control; while at the same time he has a kind of loose, yet total control. Loose enough to allow us to control our own destiny, and total enough to control the destiny of the world!

The estimated population of the world today is 7,108,847,952 and the lord has processed every single one of them, you and I, included! And not only that, but Jesus, because he was also a man, went through the same process. There was a time in Jesus's life, when the only thing little Jesus knew was that his mama had the best tasting milk in the world! Jesus found out who he was at some point in his life, but not when he wanted to know. He found out when God the Father was ready to restore his memory, as to who he was when he was just the word, before the word was made flesh. I guess you could say that Jesus had the largest case of dejavu the world has ever known!

Chapter 4

Life! Or is it?

Before I get started, I am going to quote a scripture and then ask a question. Matthew 18:9 states, "And if thine eyes offend thee, pluck it out, and cast it from thee: it is better for thee to enter into life with one eye, rather than having two eyes to be cast into hell fire." My question is this: I thought I was already in life, so what is Jesus talking about when he uses the term, enter into life?

Some people wonder how I know the things that I know. How I know about the mysteries of the Lord, and the hidden revelations in his Holy Bible. Well the answer lies in Job 33:14-16, where it states, 14 "For God speaketh once, yea twice, yet man perceiveth it not. 15 In a dream, in a vision of the night, when deep sleep falleth upon men, in slumbering upon the bed; 16 Then he openeth the ears of men, and sealeth their instruction," This is how I am enabled to know what to write! I said that, so you would understand what I mean, whenever I use the term, (The Lord said to me, the Lord asked me or the Lord caused me to understand.)

Over a period of time, the Lord said to me in my spirit, "George, you really and truly believe that this is your life that you are now living, don't you? Now to be totally honest with you, I can't remember what my answer was because, as I said, this was over a period of time. But he went ahead and pulled from my memory of the word of God, some scriptures. One was Colossians 3:2-4 in which it states, 2 "Set your affection on things above, not on things on the earth. 3 For ye are, dead, and your life is hid with Christ in God. 4 When Christ, who is our life, shall appear, then shall ye also appear with him in glory." This scripture was in conjunction with some other scriptures, which I will bring out later in this chapter. But for now, we will look at what was revealed to me in these scriptures.

In verse #2 he is saying that anything you decide to meditate on day and night will have a strong magnetic pull on your thinking, as if your thoughts were made of iron. So even though you know very little about heaven, which leaves us with much to wonder about, go ahead and wonder and meditate about heaven anyway!

In verse #3 he said that because you are a Christian, you are dead, meaning that you have drunk of the cup *that Jesus drank of! Which is what Jesus was referring to in Matthew 20:23 where it states, "And he saith unto them, Ye shall drink indeed of my cup, and be baptized with the baptism that I am baptized with:……."* The cup that Jesus drank of was, he voluntarily gave his life into the hands of God the Father, so that his life could be used for the remission of sin. Luke 23:46 states, *"And when Jesus had cried with a loud voice he said, Father, INTO THY HANDS I COMMEND MY SPIRIT:……"* This was Jesus voluntarily laying down his life, not having his life taken from him, which is his death! Also in John 10:17&18 it states, 17 *"Therefore doth my Father love me, because I lay down my life, that I might take it again. 18 No man taketh it from me, but I lay it down of myself. I have power to lay it down, and I have power to take it again. This commandment have I received of my Father."*

Next came his burial. His burial was a simple one. He was put in a grave and then the grave was SEALED. Now just because a body is placed in a grave, does not mean that the body is buried. For it to be constituted a burial, the body must be placed in the grave and the grave must be SEALED! It doesn't matter if the grave is sealed with dirt, or with a huge rock.

Last, but not least, we come to the last phase of the cup which Jesus drank from, which was his resurrection.

But before we get started on that, I want to draw your attention to the word that Jesus used to describe the entire ordeal he was about to go through. In Matthew 26:42 it states, "He went away again the second time, and prayed, saying, O my Father, if this CUP may not pass away from me, except I drink it, thy will be done." And in (John 18:11) it states, "Then said Jesus unto Peter, Put up thy sword into the sheath: the CUP which my Father hath given me, shall I not drink it?"

Let us start with the fact that the Jesus who died and was buried is not the same Jesus who was resurrected. The Jesus who died and was buried, was not weak at all, but yet and still he was nowhere near as strong as the Jesus who rose from the grave! If you think there is no difference between the Jesus who died, and the Jesus who rose, then think again. Matthew 28:18 states, "And Jesus came and spake unto them, saying, All power is given unto me in heaven and in earth."

Now before Jesus died and rose from the dead, he did not have all power in heaven and in earth. He had the same body when he rose, that he had when he was buried. The enemy would have us to believe that Jesus had the same amount of power after he rose from the dead, as he did before he died. The reason why the enemy wants us to believe there was no difference is because of the significance of this one seemingly small unimportant fact! According to the scripture, the cup Jesus drank from made him stronger!

The enemy also would have us to believe that nothing happened when we got saved, but actually what happened was;

1. Just like Christ, you voluntarily gave your life to God the Father, so that it can be used for the remission of sins. The work of all Christians is to teach people how to get rid of their past sins, and how not to commit new sins. This is called remission of sins.

2. The old you was slain by the Holy Spirit, not your flesh, but you, which means you died. What I mean when I say you is, you do not have a spirit and soul, and you ARE the combination of both spirit and soul. So it is you that died, not your body. Both spirit and soul died. This is your death! You have the same body, and the same memory, just like Jesus had the same body and the same memory. Then you were buried inside the body of Christ and sealed by the Holy Spirit until the day of delivery, or some would say baptized by the Holy Spirit, and sealed! This is your burial! Just like Christ was buried! Ephesians 4:30 states, "And grieve not the holy Spirit of God, whereby ye are sealed unto the day of redemption." The word redemption means "delivery." Then you were resurrected a new creation in Christ, behold, all things are new!

In (2nd Corinthians 5:17) it states, "Therefore if any man be in Christ, he is a new creature: old things are passed away; behold, all things are become new." But exactly what is it about me that's new? Answer, You have a new and much-much more powerful spirit! Your old spirit was weak and without strength, but your new spirit is strong enough to get you into the kingdom of Heaven, if you choose to use this God-given power to get to Heaven.

You see when Jesus died and came back alive, we called it resurrection, but when we died and came back alive, we called it born again. But they are both the same identical thing! To live one time is to be born one time: to die one time and live one more time, is to be born one more time and to be born one more time is to be born again! This is what Jesus did, and when we accepted Christ, this is what we did!

Now about power or strength we now have that we did not have before we got saved. Proof that we did not always have it is in (Romans 5:6) where it states, "For when we were yet without strength, in due time Christ died for the ungodly." Before we got saved, we did not have the strength to resist sin consistently, even if we really wanted to! Proof that we now have it is in (John 1:12) where it states, "But as many as received him, to them gave He power to become the sons of God, even to them that believe on his name:" First, so there will be no confusion, The term "Sons of God" means angels. In (Job 1:6) it states, "Now there was a day when the sons of God came to present themselves before the Lord,… … … … ."

Here are some things that you need to know about this power.

#1. The power does not cause us to be no longer dependent upon the Lord. As a matter of fact, it actually makes us more dependent on the Lord. Why? Because it not only makes it possible for us to be able to work with the Lord. But more importantly, it makes it possible for the Lord to be able to work with us according to the rules God has set for himself to abide by when it come to working with us. Because the power has within it, the ability to humble us!

#2. It is not an inherited supernatural right, but it is an inherited supernatural strength!

#3. It does not need for you to believe that it exists, in order for it to exist. Because it does exist and will continue to exist, whether you believe that it exists or not! But if you intend to use it, you must first believe that it exists. Hebrews 11:6 states, "But without faith it is impossible to please him: for he that cometh to God must believe that he is, and that he is a rewarder of them that diligently seek him."

#4. This power or strength, can only be used to do the right thing. But if you should decide to sin and go out and sin, do not say that it failed you. All that will have happened in such a case, is you will have simply decided to intentionally refuse to use the power! Jesus underwent torture and died on a cross, just to wash away your past sins, and give you the strength/ power to sin no more! Under the Old Testament a person could not enter the kingdom of heaven unless they repented of their sin, gave a sacrifice, and go and sinned no more. Under the New Testament, a person cannot enter the kingdom of heaven unless they repent of their sin, give Jesus as their sacrifice, and go and sin no more. Now if you look closely, you will see that aside from the fact that Jesus's blood washes away sins of both the Old and New testament times, the only other thing we can see that he did was saved the animals from ever again being butchered as sacrifices!

All that I have just now stated is true; but it's not the whole truth. The whole truth is God the Father did not send Jesus down here to give us what we basically already had. He sent him to give us what we did not have, but needed: strength/power! John 14:17 states, "Even the spirit of truth; whom the world cannot receive, because it seeth him not, neither knoweth him; for he dwelleth with you, and shall be in you." This is the power/strength! And it is no longer with us; it is in us who believe! The main purpose of the Holy Spirit is not to cause you to speak in tongues. The main purpose of the Holy Spirit is that it literally is your strength/power! Strength/power to do the right thing.

In the process of time, the Lord asked me: Why do you continue to sin, when you know that I will not allow you to enter the kingdom unless you stop? My answer to his question was, "I do want to stop, but for some reason I'm just not strong enough!" Then he said to me, "If I give you the strength to stop sinning, would you use it to stop?" Then I said, "Yes Lord, I would use it to stop." Then he removed the scales from my eyes, and took me to the scriptures and showed me that he had already given me the strength/power.

When I saw it, I asked him, "If I have had the power ever- since I got saved, then why haven't I been able to use it? He then said to me, "Because you didn't know that you had it!" Luke 24:49 states, "And, behold, I send the promise of my Father upon you: but tarry ye in the city of Jerusalem, until ye be endued with power from on high." The power from on high was, and still is, the Holy Spirit. Acts 2:4 states, "And they were all filled with the Holy Ghost, and began to speak with other tongues, as the spirit gave utterance."

The power that was sent from the Father was the Holy Spirit. But for some reason this is where mankind's understanding gets derailed! We look for all of the fruits of the spirit except the power/strength. Without the power/strength, we will experience little if any success at all, consistently utilizing the rest of the gifts of the spirit. After being born again, of God this time means that we now have the benefit of Hereditary traits. Supernatural spiritual faith-activated strength/power, whether we know we have it or not!

Now as I said before, when we became a Christian we literally drank of the same cup that Jesus drank of. We died, were buried and was resurrected, just like Christ. Not only that, all this happened to us in the twinkling of an eye, in the moment that you got saved! The moment you believed is the moment you got saved, which is also the moment you were changed! In (1 Corinthians 15:51&52) it states, 51 "Behold, I shew you a mystery; We shall not all sleep, but we shall all be changed, 52 In a moment, in the twinkling of an eye, at the last trump: for the trump shall sound, and the dead shall be raised incorruptible, and we shall be changed." This is exactly how we were changed to what we are now.

What I'm about to tell you is going to be difficult for some to understand, and easy for others, but Jesus's death, burial and resurrection also took place in the twinkling of an eye! The twinkling of an eye is a term used to describe approximately 20% less than half of a second of time, which is the amount of time it takes to blink your eye. I really cannot think of any other way to say it than to just say it, so here we go. One thousand years of man's time = one day of God's time! 41 years and eight months of man's time = one hour of God's time! 8 months and 10 days of man's time = one minute of God's time! 4 days and 4 hours of man's time = one second of God's time! 2 days and 2 hours of man's time = half of a second of God's time!

The scripture states that Jesus died the ninth hour, on a Friday. The ninth hour means he died at three p.m. Friday during the daytime. From 3 p.m. Friday, until 12 O'clock midnight is a total of 9 hours. He was dead the entire day of Saturday, which is another 24 hours. When you put them together is comes to 33 hours. The scripture states that he rose before the sun came up Sunday morning. So that means that he rose around 6:00 or 6:30 a.m. Sunday morning, which is another 6 or 6½ hours. Now when you add up all the hours that Jesus was actually dead, it will come to approximately 39½ hours: and 39½ hours to God the Father is a little bit less than half of a second, which is a twinkling of the eye to God All Mighty!

Colossians 3:4 states, "When Christ, who is our life, shall appear, then shall ye also appear with him in glory." In verse #4 He used the word appear, which is the direct opposite of the word disappear. So what the verse is saying is real life is in a place where you can see, not only Jesus for the first time, but you can also see yourself for the first time. Notice that two things become visible in this verse; Jesus and You. Also in verse #4 it states "Christ, who is our life." Now if the scripture is true, and Christ is our life, and no one alive today has ever seen Christ; then that means no one alive today has ever seen LIFE! So the Lord asked me, "do I think that he, the Lord, is real?" And I said, "Yes, there is no doubt in my mind that you are real." Then he said, "If this is real life, and you by your own confession say that I am real, then why is it that you cannot see me?"

Well, to that statement I did not have an answer. Then he said, "George, are you real?" And I said, "Of course I am real", then he said, "Yes you are real, but if this is real life, why can't you at least see your own self? You can see the body that you live in, but you can't see you!" When he put it to me that way, I scratched my head for a little while. I then said, "You know something, I been wondering about that, ever since you explained to me that the body I live in belongs to me, but it is not me." Oh ya, I forgot when he said, "If I say that this is life where I am, and George you say that that is life where you are, then why can I see you but you can't see me?"

Then he asked me a series of questions, based on what the Holy Spirit had already taught me about time. Which lead to yet another, more conclusive question. So he said, "George, how long is a day to the Lord?" I said," What the Lord calls a day, man calls it one thousand years." Then he said, "If a day equals to a thousand years, then what does one hour of the Lord's time equal to?" Then I said, "One hour of the Lord's time, equals to 41years and 8months of man's time." Then he asked me how many years does the average person live? And I said, "The average person lives about 80 years, but every now-and-then, someone lives to be 120 years old. Then he said to me, "Let me get this straight, If the average person lives about 80 years, and every now-and-then 120 years, then according to the Lord's time, the average person only lives about two hours, and every-now-then someone lives close to three hours." Then I said, "Well if you put that way, then yes, we do only live two or three hours!"

Then he ask me the question that he had been leading up to all the time, which was, "George, if this is real life, then don't you think that it would last a little longer than two or three hours?" Then I said, "Lord, you are right, there is no way this can be real life, if it only lasts *two or three hours." Is it simulated life? No! Then what? Actually it is only a very-very-very, tiny sample: a sample that is identical to a dream. However, it is not a dream; only, identical to a dream!*

Now remember, this was all communicated to me over a period of time: In other words, the Lord can reveal something to you in 1992, reveal something else to you in 1997, and then reveal yet something else in 2014. Then wait until 2015 to reveal to you that the 1992, 1997 and 2014's revelations where actually different parts of one conversation that you were unknowingly participating in with the Lord. A conversation that was impossible to recognize as a conversation, until the Holy Spirit took each revelation and arranged them in the order that would cause me to recognize them as an actual conversation with the Lord himself!

This reminds me of two scriptures; one of them is Matthew 13:52, which states, "Then said he unto them, therefore every scribe which is instructed unto the kingdom of heaven is like unto a man that is an householder, which bringeth forth out of his treasure things new and old." (The word scribe, 2,000 years ago meant a person who writes books or documents by hand as a profession, and helps keep track of records.) The other one is Isaiah 28:10, which states, "For precept must be upon precept, precept upon precept; line upon line, line upon line; here a little, and there a little:" It is the here a little, and there a little part, that reminds me of what it is like working with the Lord directly.

The spirit then communicated a question to me. The question was, "George how long does a dream usually last?" My reply was, "I don't really know, ah-ah two or three hours I guess!" Then the Spirit communicated two parallel questions to me, which were; "If, when you are Asleep dreaming and you find 1million dollars in a bag, can you take the bag with you when you wake up from the dream? And if, in your lifetime, you save up 1million dollars in a bank, and you die, can you take the money that really is in the bank and really is your money; can you take that money with you?" My answers were, "No and no!"

Then the Spirit communicated to me another question. "Is there anything at all that a person can carry with them from a dream to this world or from this world to either Heaven or Hell?" My answer was, "No!" Then the Spirit said to me, "George, you have answered all of the questions correctly, except this last question. The reason why, is because there is one thing, and one thing only, that you can carry from your dream to the world you are in, as well as from this world to Heaven. That one thing is your MEMORY! I, the Lord, can warn you in a dream to stay at home tomorrow, instead of using the ticket you bought to fly to California. Then when you wake up, you take the only thing you could take with you from the dream you just had, which is the Memory. And take heed to the memory of the dream, and cancel your trip. Then two hours later a news flash comes on the television announcing that the plane you were going to ride has crashed to the ground, killing everyone on board! The memory you took from your dream, saved your life.

When you die and leave this world, and stand before the Judge of Heaven and Earth; Although you may say, or wish to say many things, there will be no need, because the Judge of Heaven and Earth will use your own memory to judge you. It will either save your life or condemn you to the Lake of Fire!

Your memories are not written from the books that will be opened on that day! The books that will be opened on that day are written from your memories! If your memories show LOVE, MERCY, OBEDIENCE and FORGIVENESS, then that is what you will be judged by. If your memories show otherwise, then that is what you will be judged by. You can remember telling a lie, but it is not possible to remember a lie, because a lie never occurred!

The supporting scriptures for things said in this chapter are as follows: The confirmation that the understanding of days and times are keys to wisdom! (Psalm 90:12), "So teach us to number our days, that we may apply our hearts unto wisdom." The confirmation that 1,000 years of man's time = one day of the Lord's time. (2nd Peter 3:8) "But, beloved, be not ignorant of this one thing, that one day is with the Lord as a thousand years, and a thousand years as one day." Confirmation that when a 1,000 years have passed, that the passing of that 1,000 years, God calls yesterday. Just as a man calls the passing of 24 hours yesterday! (Psalm 90:4), "For a thousand years in thy sight are but as yesterday when it is past, and as a watch in the night." The confirmation that the Spirit compares man's time on the earth, as well as his entire life, to a dream: the KJV uses the term (as a sleep-meaning-dreaming) (Psalm 90: 5&6 +RSV) 5."Thou carriest them away as with a flood; they are as a sleep:" (means it is like they are dreaming), (or it is like they are living a dream) in the morning they are like grass which growth up.

6. *In the morning it flourisheth, and growth up; in the evening it is cut down, and withereth up." Notice that in verse #6 man's life is depicted as being born in the morning and dying in the evening; meaning that from where the narrator is sitting, mankind dies the same day that they are born! In order to view mankind's life span, which ranges on the average from 70 to 100*

years, as beginning and ending on the same day; the viewer himself, clearly has a different understanding of the word day than the understanding that mankind has of the word day! So where the narrator is sitting, 24 hours is nowhere near being considered a day. So yes, we are alive, but is this life?

Chapter 5

Identifying the Heart

Many people in the world today do not know the difference between their mind and their heart. Some don't know if there really is a difference. In (Proverbs 4:23) it states, "Keep thy heart with all diligence; for out of it are the issues of life." In this verse wisdom is instructing all of mankind to guard their heart at all cost, because all things dealing with life come out of it.

A good way to identify your heart would be this; let's say you are a man and you are watching a movie with a few other guys, in one big room. And the movie has a very sad part where someone dies. Now this is a room full of guys, and men do not allow other men to see them cry. You feel yourself about to shed a tear. So immediately you use your mind to tell yourself that this is not real, this is just a movie. And that you are not going to let the guys see you crying. That is a direct *order! But your eyes fill up with water and your mind says to yourself, "I can't believe it; I'm crying."*

When you analyze the situation as to what just took place, you will find that your mind tried to stop your heart from crying, but your mind got ran, flat-slap over, by your heart.

Here is another example to further increase your understanding of the strength and power of your heart, as opposed to the strength and power of your mind. Let's say your heart and mind were both able to lift heavy weights; your mind is strong enough to lift 495lbs, and your heart is only strong enough to lift 490lbs. When you look at it this way, you would be tempted to say the mind is stronger than the heart. But there is a problem. The mind can indeed lift 495lbs, which is five pounds more than the heart can lift. But it can only lift it two times per-day, whereas the heart can only lift 490lbs, but it can lift it 25 times per-day. So after closer examination you can see that the real work-horse is the heart!

Before we go any further, I think we need to first dissect and analyze the only scripture in the Bible that brings this vital subject to the attention of the world! In Proverbs 4:23 it states, "Keep thy heart with all diligence" (which means protect it at all cost) "for out of it are the issues of life." (This means because every single thing to do with life, both temporary and eternal, will come out of it.)

The first thing we need to look at is the fact that the narrator addresses the reader, which is what you and I are, as thy, which means, your. When you see the word (your) in a sentence, it indicates you as the owner. You are the owner of whatever immediately follows the word your; whether it be an object or a situation, it belongs to you.

Next we should focus on the fact that in the second half of the verse, the narrator refers to the heart as (it). By him referring to the heart as (it), instead of referring to the heart as (you), he is indicating that your heart and you are two different things, existing together within the same body. Now it goes without saying that the narrator is talking (about) the heart. So the only thing left to do is to properly identify (what), as well as (who) the narrator is talking (to). The narrator is talking to your mind and addressing it as you! So the narrator is instructing the mind to protect the heart.

But that leads to another question; doesn't it? Protect it from what? The mind is the one that does all the fresh thinking. It filters through all new thoughts and thinks quickly on the spot for you. Your mind is able to convince you that it is who you really are, if you have not yet come to the knowledge, and the understanding as to who you really are.

It can also convince others that it is who you are, if they haven't known you long enough to know who you really are. You can be thinking in your mind, that you do not love money; but if the price is right, and nobody is watching, you wind up doing the same thing every time! You say to yourself; who will know the difference? Besides, this is not who I really am. >>> "Or is it?"<<< Well to start with, I think we had better answer the question, "Protect it from what?"

It is the mind's responsibility to keep the heart from being exposed to, for example, the use of profanity. Not so much the being around it and hearing it, as the act of using it. Being around it and hearing it, is dangerous to the mind, because constant exposure to (cussing), as we call it in Mississippi, will increase the likelihood that the mind will sooner or later try it. When the mind makes the decision to go ahead and use profanity the first 10, 15 or maybe even 20 times, the heart may, or may not be safe. But by the time the mind makes the decision to use it 10 or 15 more times, it is too late! At that point, the mind will have sown it into the heart.

The mind, from that point on, will no longer have to make the decision as to whether or not to use profanity.

Because the heart will both make the decision to do it, and carry it out, for the remainder of your life. Unless the mind, at some point realizes you are condemned to the lake of fire whenever this life is over; because the heart has grabbed hold of something that is not allowed in the kingdom, and the mind is not strong enough to make the heart let go of it. Because the mind is just a little bit stronger than the heart, it is able to force the heart to let go of it, two or three times in a day maybe. But the persistence of the heart, proved to be much-much more than the mind could deal with!

So the mind discovers yet another shocking revelation, which is, it does not possess the power to simply over rule the heart.....and never did! Most of the minds in this world either have accidently created a monster that they do not know how to control, or they are in the process of accidently creating a monster that they do not know how to control!

The solution, however, will come later in this chapter; but for now we will learn more about both the heart and the mind. One thing you should know about the heart is that it is not curious of its own doing, nor does it conduct experiments, of its own doing. That is a function of the mind for the most part, at least initially. What I mean by that is, the heart will not allow any kind of conduct, nor any kind of trend of thought, or pattern of thinking inside it, until it is repeated enough times to become what is called a (habit.) Because the mind is very seldom curious about any given thing, that is (out) of its realm of possibility, a sufficient number of times to become what the heart considers a habit, impossible curiosities remain the work of the mind only.

But when the mind is curious about something that (is) in its realm of possibility, enough times for the heart to consider it a habit, and then the heart will take it in. And if by chance the person solves the mystery of their curiosity, by going ahead and finally doing the thing that they've been curious about for so long, they will still find themselves curious about the thing that is no longer a mystery. At least for a small period of time, and then it will go away.

This is a classic case of the mind unknowingly reprogramming the heart! The mind unknowingly taught the heart to be curious about a specific thing. So the heart activated the mind's curiosity toward that particular thing, automatically, every time the conditions were right. What I mean by, (when the conditions were right) is..…If a person relished in their curiosity, in the form of daydreaming every time the busyness of each day slowed down, or every time they walked out on to their balcony; then those two situations are the times in which the heart considers (the right conditions). So when the mind experiences curiosity, mysteriously being forced upon it pertaining to what used to be, but is no longer a curiosity, it ends the outdated curiosity by reminding itself by visualizing in their mind, the moment when he or she finally experienced the activity that they used to be so curious about. When they do that, they mentally re-witness the solving of the mystery. The mind does this every time the heart does what it does, and slowly but surely the mind reprograms the heart's mind and the heart's mind actually stops itself eventually, from doing it anymore. Yet it does not forget, neither does the mind, unless you live long enough to no longer be able to remember it any more.

People my age and older can remember a time when one of their parents would ask them, "Have you studied your homework yet? And our answer would be "Yes, mama, I know it by heart now!" Now that I am older, I think back to those days, and say to myself, "We just didn't know how close to the truth we were when we said those few, seemingly innocent words, "I learned it by heart."

Jesus in your mind, or Jesus on your mind, is a good thing! But if he never makes it to the place inside you that he is struggling to get to, then on the Last Day, as much as he would like to, he is not going to be able to safely deliver you home to the kingdom! In (Revelation

3:20) it states, "Behold, I stand at the door, and knock: if any man hear my voice, and open the door, I will come in to him, and I will sup with him, and he with me." The door Jesus is speaking of is not your mind, it is your heart! To guide a car to the place you want to go to, you have to sit behind the steering wheel. Having Jesus as a passenger in your car is the same as having him in or on your mind, which is a good start. But the only way you are going to get to where you are trying to go is to let him have the steering wheel. In other words, let him into your heart. (Unless you already know how to get there!)

You have to take in mind also, the fact that unclean spirits also know how to manipulate both the mind and the heart, and their number one objective is to gain and maintain control of the heart!

Many of us seem to see the mind as a control tower, and it is, but it is not the main control tower! The main control tower has the power to overrule the other control tower. But the control tower does not have the power to overrule the main control tower! Your mind does not have a mind of its own, because it is a mind. But that is not the case when it comes to your heart. Your heart actually has a mind of its own! When these two minds do not see eye-to-eye, then we have, not just A-problem, but THE PROBLEM! This is the problem

Identifying the Heart

Jesus's brother spoke about in the book of James. In (James 1:8) it states "A double minded man is unstable in all his ways."

The thinking done with the mind is original for the most part. But the thinking done by the heart's mind is not original. It never was and never will be. The thinking done by your heart's mind is what is called programmed thinking! It was programmed to think the way that it thinks. And it was programmed to think the thoughts that it thinks, and it was done so by your mind.

Let me pause to say this; your mind is a built-in entertainment center, with fast forward, pause, rewind, instant porn, and you don't even need a remote! When we are young, we humans, for the most part, unknowingly use our minds to program our hearts to participate in, and meditate on, things that we later in life find out will disqualify us from being able to enter the kingdom of heaven!

The mind is very, very dangerous, and it is not a toy. Yet when we are young, we can't think of anything we would rather play with more than the mind! There is a verse in the Bible that I want to draw your attention to, actually it is a part of a verse. In (Genesis 8-part of-:21) it states "… … ..for the imagination of man's heart is evil from his youth;... ... " Let's say you have a person who is incarcerated for 10 or 20 years, and lives through it all and is finally set free and still in his right mind. If you ask him how he was able to do that much time, without losing his mind? If he gives that question deep-deep thought and is perfectly honest, he will tell you he used his imagination almost every single day to take himself to places he could not go, and to do things he could not do, both good and evil: And one day 10 or 20 years later, they told him he could actually go home!

The next couple of scriptures I am going to quote are on a note that you would call a negative-note, but it brings out a very positive truth. Proverbs 23:6&7 states, "Eat thou not the bread of him that hath an evil eye, neither desire thou his dainty meats: 7. For as he thinketh in his heart, so is he: Eat and drink, saith he to thee; but his heart is not with thee." Two points are being made in these verses. #1. The mind can direct the mouth to say any number of things. #2. The true essence of who a person is the ongoing thought process of the heart's mind; not the mind, but the heart's mind! In other words, as it is in the process, or actual motion of thinking in its own established style of thought, that is who a person really is. UNDERSTANDING WHAT I AM SAYING IS YOUR ONLY CHANCE OF EVER KNOWING WHO YOU REALLY ARE!

Identifying the Heart

The reason why I said thinking in-motion is because motion is evidence or proof of the existence of life and you are a living existence. You can say it, just as your father in heaven said it to Moses, "I am that I am", which means, I exist! I have already earlier in this book, stated that we cannot see ourselves. But because of this knowledge, we can at least begin to understand ourselves!

Now we come to the solution. The reason there is a solution to this seemingly impossible situation is because we, as Christians, have supernatural spiritual strength, plus we have access to supernatural counsel. The supernatural spiritual strength you have was inherited from Jesus when you sacrificed yourself to Christ. In the twinkling of an eye, you were slain by the Holy Spirit, sealed inside the body of Christ also by the Holy Spirit, and then resurrected. This is commonly referred to as born again. You have the same body and mind just like Jesus did. In fact his body still had holes in it. But you do not have the same spirit, because your old spirit literally died. This is why the scriptures states, in 2nd Corinthians, "Therefore If any man be in Christ, he is a new creature: old things are passed away; behold, all things are become new."

The spirit you now have come out of the body you were born from this time, which was inside of Christ's body. So you inherited his supernatural spiritual strength. Before this we were weak. Romans 5:6 states, "For when we were yet without strength, in due time Christ died for the ungodly." This verse proves that there was a time when we had no power/strength.

But all that changed. John 1:12 states, "But as many as received him, to them gave he power/strength to become the sons of God, even to them that believed on his name:"

You cannot use it to walk on water or raise the dead, but you can use it for its intended purpose. Its purpose is to equip you with more than enough spiritual strength to do the right thing on a consistent basis, whether you use it or not, as well as whether you believe you have it or not!

If you can do that you will become one of the Sons or Daughters of God. You can also choose to not use it at will. You have it in you, but you simply didn't know that you had it. Let's say you come from a family of very strong men, but you were adopted and didn't know it. So you think that you can only lift about 275 lbs. most of your life until one day you meet your real grandfather. You and he talk and he tells you that you come from a long line of exceptionally strong men. He also tells you that his great grandfather, his grandfather, his father, he himself and his son, which is your daddy, could all lift more than 600 lbs. when they were your age, and for sure, he knows that you can do it because it is in you. As a result you get a few instructions from your granddaddy on how to work out, and before you know it, after about a 1 ½ years, you are lifting just a little over 620 lbs. All because you had it in you but didn't know it. To keep saying you cannot stop sinning is the equivalent of saying that you can only lift 275 lbs.

First, the truth does not need for you to believe that it is truth in order for it to continue being the truth! However, for the truth to work for us, we have to #1 believe the truth and #2 act upon it. It is not enough to simply believe. Simply believing is called believing. Acting upon what you believe is called FAITH! Hebrews 11:6 states, "But without faith it is impossible to please him: for he that cometh to God must believe that he is, and that he is a rewarder of those that diligently seek him."

The word faith means trust. I can truly believe you will take good care of my car, and at the same time, not trust you with it. But the moment I give you the keys, is the moment I trust you with it! That is the only definition of the word Faith!

In (1st Corinthians 2:16) it states, "For who hath known the mind of the Lord," (God the Father) "that he may instruct him? But we have the mind of Christ." When the scripture states "we have the mind of Christ", it means, we have access to the mind of Christ! As Christians, we are not on the outside of the body of Christ, because if we were on the outside of the body, then we would not have access to the mind of Christ. Because we are on the inside of the body of Christ that means that our minds have access to "the mind of Christ!" This is where we can connect to both supernatural strength, as well as supernatural counsel, which by the way, is how I am able to write this very book that you are now reading!

We must use our mind to reprogram our heart's mind, through Christ! This is exactly what Paul instructed us to do in Romans 12:2 "...: but be ye transformed by the renewing of your mind,…… .." But never lose focus. You must take your faith and connect it to your focus, and try never to allow the two to separate. If your focus somehow gets separated from your faith, then simply refocus, as many times as necessary. Your faith is in this one thing, and that is that the strength you need in order to focus long enough to reprogram your heart does indeed exist, and it exist in you simply because you are in Christ!

Identifying the Heart 77

In many cases, the Lord himself intentionally takes more time than what you consider necessary to deliver your request, in order to create patience in you. Because patience is the only thing in this world that can increase the strength of your faith! You see in (Philippians 4:13) it states, "I can do all things through Christ which strengthened me." But we see in Matthew 14:29-31 that faith was present and working just fine, until Peter's focus was distracted, which allowed doubt to manifest itself and then he begin to sink. Matthew 14:29-31 it states, 29. "And he said, Come. And when Peter was come down out of the ship, he walked on the water, to go to Jesus. 30. But when he saw the wind boisterous, he was afraid; and beginning to sink, he cried, saying, Lord, save me. 31. And immediately Jesus stretched forth his hand, and caught him, and said unto him, O thou of little faith, wherefore didst thou doubt?"

Now when it comes to stepping out on faith, I can tell you from experience that the first thing that is going to happen is it's going to look like it is not working. Or it will look like it is working just fine, until it starts looking like it is not working. So when that happens, don't go running to the Lord, talking about, it looks like it is not working. Because the Lord, through this book, has already told you that it was going to look exactly like that, sooner or later. He also already told you that the reason it will look like that, is to distract you long enough for you to lose focus, so doubt can take away your expectation! Positive-faith is simply called Faith, but negative-faith is called Doubt! So the outcome of any request, provided the Lord allows is always according to your faith! This truth is hidden in the statement Jesus made in (Matthew 9:29) "Then touched he their eyes, saying, According to your faith be it unto you." The conclusion to this entire chapter is this. To successfully use your mind to reprogram your heart's mind, you must identify the difference between the thinking of your mind and the thinking of your heart's mind. If it is new thoughts, or new thinking, then identify that as the thoughts or thinking of your MIND! If it is old thoughts or old thinking, then you identify that as the old, recurring thoughts or thinking of your HEART'S MIND!

All recurring thoughts are not evil; so the only thinking you will be reprogramming is the evil ones. The definition of resisting the devil is this: recognize the beginning of an evil thought, and immediately replace it with a pleasant, clean thought! What works for me is, I think about playing with a little child, making them burst-out giggling, and I stay in that thought or way of thinking until I feel it is safe to return my thinking to whatever I was doing before I was attacked by evil thought!

To many this method will be considered a revelation, but in reality it is only the result of trying (Philippians 4:8) to see if it worked, and it did. The Bible is your sword, but this is your (only) shield. A soldier may be an expert with his sword, but he will not last long in battle without his shield! In (Philippians 4:8) it states, "Finally, brethren, whatsoever things are true, whatsoever things are honest, whatsoever things are just, whatsoever things are pure, whatsoever things are lovely, whatsoever things are of good report; if there be any virtue, if there be any praise, THINK ON THESE THINGS." When you see a small portion of an evil thought forming in your heart's mind, and use your mind to stop it, and replace it: do not consider yourself as having sinned. You may ask the Lord to forgive you, if you allowed yourself to see a little too much of the lustful thought before you used your shield to block it out of your mind. But if you blocked the thought as soon as you recognized it to be evil, you have not sinned. It was not half of a thought, nor a whole thought. It was only a notion!

The only way for a soldier in battle to block the enemy's sword from striking him is for him to first see and recognize the enemy's blade coming towards him. Is he wrong for having first seen, and recognized the blade, and then blocked it with his shield? No! Then neither are you wrong if you have to see a small portion of an evil thought in order to recognize that you have to block and replace the thought. God would not have given us minds if there was no way to control them.

Chapter 6

Once Saved, Always Saved, Yes Or No?

Well it all depends on what a person's understanding of what the word "saved" means. The Webster dictionary defines it as "preservation from danger or loss." In the book of (Jude 1:1) it states, "Jude, the servant of Jesus Christ, and brother of James, to them that are sanctified by God the Father, and preserved in Jesus Christ, and called:" The Webster dictionary defines the word preserve as "to save from decay: as by the use of sugar, salt, etc., as to preserve fruit." So when a person says he or she is saved, all they are really saying is that they have been placed inside the body of Christ and sealed by the Holy Spirit. Not forever, but they are sealed until the Day of Judgment, at which time they will be judged like everyone else!

Once a person is saved, he or she cannot be saved again as long as they are alive in the flesh, nor can he or she become un-saved as long as they are alive in the flesh. Ephesians 4:30 states, "And grieve not the Holy Spirit of God, whereby ye are sealed unto the day of redemption."

The word unto means until, and the word redemption means to deliver. So what the scripture is really saying, is that all Christians are sealed inside the body of Christ, not forever, but until the day of deliverance.

It is the same as when a woman is pregnant with more than one child. Let's just say she has triplets sealed inside her. The children will remain sealed inside the mother until she goes to the hospital to deliver them. Now just as the children cannot remain sealed inside the mother forever, we as Christians will not remain sealed inside the body of Christ forever! Many of us who are sealed in the body of Christ are in Death, whether (dead/asleep) or alive and breathing. You may ask, how can we, as Christians. be in a location known as Death, if we are sealed inside the body of Christ? The answer is: (EXAMPLE) The woman who went to the hospital to deliver triplets, delivers three children. Two of the children are healthy and alive, but one child is delivered dead.

Before I go any further, I think it is best that I explain the word DEATH. Death does not mean that a person is no longer living. It means they are no longer living in the same world that we are living in. So then if someone you know dies, it means they have been separated from you, to live somewhere else. With that being said, we now know that the word Death means separate.

Inside the body of Christ, there is light and there is darkness. If a saved person living in the body of Christ, and walking in the light, decides to SEPARATE from the light and enter the darkness by returning to a life of sin. If he dies while he is still separated; separate means Death. So that means that although he is still in the body of Christ, he is separated to a location called DEATH! The thing about death that makes it so deceiving is the fact that we are alive and breathing and walking and talking and having fun, so we say to ourselves ,"How can I be dead if I am alive?" The reason the woman had Death in her womb is because one of the children became entangled in its umbilical cord and was cut off from the flow of nutrition it needed in order to fully mature. Or you might prefer to use the words fully develop, which brought about the child's DEATH!

Likewise we as Christians are inside the body of Christ, waiting to be
Delivered into the kingdom of Heaven. But if while we wait, we decide to refuse the flow of Spiritual nutrition, which flows from Christ into us, (by continuing to

live in sin) it is then that we stop maturing and enter into DEATH. The scripture does not say that the wages of sin WAS death; instead, it says the wages of sin IS death.

Romans 6:23 states, "For the wages of sin IS death; but the gift of God is eternal life through Jesus Christ our Lord." Many preachers and teachers in the world today teach that, since there is no way to become unsaved as long as you are alive in this fleshly body, then there is no way for a believer to burn in Hell once he or she dies. Well on that note they are correct, to a certain extent. Because it is true that a believer in fact cannot go to the fires of hell when he or she dies. But the reason is because when Jesus died on the cross, he went into the fires of hell itself, and when he left, he was never to return. This was done because it is not possible to take on the full punishment for a sinner, unless you burn in the fires of hell also, and Jesus paid the full price.

I said all that to say this, if you are a Christian, you live and die inside the body of Christ. Since he will never again enter into the fires of hell, being that we are inside him, that means we also cannot go into the fires of hell. We can only go where he goes, and he is never going into the fires of hell again. But that does not mean we are not going to be cast into the Lake of Fire.

There is a big difference between Hell, Death and the lake of fire: Hell and death are temporary locations, but the lake of fire is a permanent location. Hell is where the non-believers who die in their sins go. Death is where the (believers /Christians) go who die in their sins. There will be some who will argue as to whether or not death is literally a location, but the scripture speaks for itself. In the book of (Revelation 20:13&14) it states, 13 "And the sea gave up the dead which were in it; and Death and Hell delivered up the dead which were in them:"(The key word is them, which is plural, meaning more than one. Now we know and confess that the sea is a location, and we know and confess that hell is a location. Why? Because these two locations gave up the dead that were in them, so why is it that many of us refuse to confess that Death is also a location, because it also gave up the dead that where in it! "and they were judged every man according to their works." 14 "And Death and Hell were cast into the lake of fire. This is the second death."

In (1st John 3:14) it states, "We know that we have passed from death unto life because we love the brethren. He that loveth not his brother abideth in death." The word abideth means to dwell or to live in. So if we do not love our brother, it means we are living in a location called Death. Now note this, Death is the loca-

tion, but Dead is the condition! A good example would be Matthew 8:21&22 which states, 21 "And another of his disciples said unto him, Lord suffer me first to go and bury my father. 22 But Jesus said unto him, follow me; and let the dead bury their dead." The condition of the disciple's father was physically dead, but the condition of the people whom Jesus suggested should bury his father was "spiritually dead." A person cannot abide in any location unless the location itself does indeed exist!

In the book of (James 5:19&20) it states, 19 "Brethren, if any of you do err from the truth, and one convert him;" (If you will notice, he used the word brethren, which means that he is referring to all Christians. Then he uses the word you, meaning if any of us Christians do stray from the righteous path.) 20 "Let him know, that he which converteth the sinner from the error of his way shall save a soul from death, and shall hide a multitude of sins." If you will notice, the writer did not say, "shall save a soul from hell." Instead he said, "shall save a soul from Death."

The apostle Paul stated in (1st Corinthians 9:27), "But I keep under my body, and bring it into subjection: lest that by any means, when I have preached to others, I myself should be a castaway." What Paul is saying is that he keeps his flesh from sinning, because if he does not keep himself from sinning, then he himself will be found unfit to enter the kingdom of heaven, even though he preaches the gospel to others! This was and is a message to the believer. On the subject of messages to the believer we will go to Mark 16:17&18 where it states, 17 "And these signs shall follow them that believe; In my name shall they cast out devils; they shall speak with new tongues; 18 They shall take up serpents; and if they drink any deadly thing, it shall not hurt them; they shall lay hands on the sick, and they shall recover." These are things only the believer can do in Jesus's name.

But look at what the scripture says will happen to the believers who perform these miracles in Jesus name, yet they themselves continue living in sin! In (Matthew 7:21) it states, "Not every one that saith unto me, Lord, Lord, shall enter the kingdom of heaven; but he that doeth the will of my father which is in heaven." What Jesus is saying in this verse is that not everyone who has accepted Jesus Christ as their Lord and Savior will enter into the kingdom of heaven! In (Matthew 7:22&23) it states, 22"Many will say to me in that day, Lord, Lord, have we not prophesied in thy name? And in thy name have cast out devils? And in thy name done many wonderful works? 23 And then will I profess unto them, I never knew you"

The statement, "I never knew you," does not mean he never got to know you as a person; because in Jeremiah 1:5 it states, "Before I formed thee in the belly I knew thee;……." This means that he knew what our name would be before we were born, he knew how our lives would go if we obey him and he knew how our lives would go if we disobey him. The answer to what he means by the statement, "I never knew you", can be found in Genesis 4:1 which states, "And Adam knew Eve his wife; and she conceived, and bare Cain, said, I have gotten a man from the Lord;" This means Eve allowed Adam to enter into her and she conceived: likewise, we all, as

Christians, must allow Christ to enter into us! Just because we have entered into Christ does not mean that he has entered into us! In (John 10:37&38) it states, 37 "If I do not the works of my father, believe me not. 38 But if I do, though you believe not me, believe the works: that ye may know, and believe, that the father is in me, and I in him." Though an unborn child is inside its mother, the mother is also flowing into the unborn child; the child is in her and she is in the child, and it is in this way that the two are one. John 10:30 states, "I and my father are one."

When we go into Christ our salvation is not yet secure, it has only begun. When Christ comes into us, then, and then only is our salvation secure, and even at that point we are not yet all the way in the clear! The reason why is because it is not enough to simply make it to a place where you are safe and secure. Once you get there, you have to also remain there! In (John 15:6&7) it states, 6 "If a man abide not in me, he is cast forth as a branch, and is withered; and men gather them and cast them into the fire, and they are burned. 7 If ye abide in me, and my words abide in you, ye shall ask what ye will, and it shall be done unto you."

In (Revelation 3:20) it states, "Behold, I stand at the door, and knock: if any man hear my voice, and open the door, I will come in to him, and will sup with him, and he with me." It is in this way that we become one with Christ, and Christ is one with the Father, causing us to become one with the Father also. John 14:23 states, "Jesus answered and said unto him, if a man love me, he will keep my words: and my Father will love him, and we will come unto him, and make our abode with him." And in (2nd Corinthians 5:19) it states, "To wit, that God was in Christ, reconciling the world unto himself, not imputing their trespasses unto them: and hath committed unto us the word of reconciliation."

At this point I feel compelled to bring out more facts, that when brought together, should make your understanding crystal clear. One scripture states the fact that some will never taste of death, and the other scripture states that some will not taste of death until the lord returns. The point to remember is the word "until," meaning that they will taste death; it's just that they won't taste it until he returns. In (John 8:51&52) it states, 51"Verily, verily, I say unto you, if a man keep my saying, he will never see death." (Now we know that he is not referring to physical death, because 11 of his apostles kept his sayings, and all of them at this point have died the physical death, so we know he is referring to what is called the second death.) 52 "Then said the Jews unto him, now we know that thou hast a devil. Abraham is dead, and the prophets; and thou sayest, If a man keep my saying, he shall never taste of death." In (Mark 9:1) it states, "And he said unto them, Verily I say unto you, That there be some that stand here, which shall not taste of death, till they have seen the kingdom of God come with power."

The reason he said that was because, there were standing there with him at the time, people who were believers and also some who would become believers. However, they were going to return to a life of sin, and in doing so, they would give up their opportunity to live forever in the kingdom of heaven. Because when once a man confesses, and believes, he then becomes automatically what we call saved, and is sealed inside the body of Christ by the Holy Spirit. Because it is your belief that saves you, but it is your conduct that determines whether or not you will be accepted into the kingdom of heaven!

I mentioned it before, but I will mention it again, it is your behavior after you get saved that determines whether or not you get to live in the kingdom of heaven forever. In (1st Corinthians 9:27) Paul states, "But I keep under my body, and bring it into subjection: lest that by any means, when I have preached to others, I myself be a castaway." Now if Paul, who taught us all we know about salvation, states that even though he is saved, if he does not conduct himself the way a Christian must conduct himself, even he will not be allowed to live in the kingdom of heaven eternally! (By the way, the word castaway in this verse means disqualified.)

So the question is, How did so many so-called Bible scholars and theologians come to the conclusion that once you get saved, there is no way you can become disqualified to live in heaven eternally? The answer to that question can be found in the next three groups of scriptures I am about to either introduce, or reintroduce to you.

The first group is in (2nd Corinthians 11:13-15) where Paul states, 13 "For such are false apostles, deceitful workers, transforming themselves into the apostles of Christ. 14 And no marvel; for Satan himself is transformed into an angel of light. 15 Therefore it is no great thing if his ministers also be transformed as the ministers of righteousness; whose end shall be according to their works."

The office of a shepherd receives much respect. The office of a shepherd receives a great deal of honor and attention. But the biggest problem in our world today is that the office of shepherd makes a lot of money. There are many, not all, but many preachers in the world today who were not called by the Lord to preach the gospel. We are all called to hear the gospel and to obey it!

But many decide within themselves to make themselves preachers, often because their fathers or some other family member either is or was a preacher. So they go to Bible College and become just that. Some do it for the attention, some for the respect, some for the money and some for two out of three of these reasons. Some do it for all three reasons. But the worst case of all is when a man is either truly called by the Lord to preach the gospel, and refuses to do so. Or he, not she, is called and begins to preach the gospel because he is in love with the Lord, but somewhere down the line he falls more in love with the money or popularity. This can compel him to exchange his sometimes unpopular message of the truth for a more popular and more lucrative message. Which I call, not simply (a lie), but rather THE LIE! I call it The Lie, because all those who tell it, tell the same lie; which is once you get saved there is no way you can burn in the lake of fire.

The second group of scriptures that provide answers as to why so many bible scholars and theologians have come to the conclusion that your conduct after getting saved cannot disqualify you from being able to enter the kingdom, is found in (2nd Thessalonians 2:11&12) where Paul states, 11 "And for this cause God shall send them strong delusion, that they should (BELIEVE A LIE): 12 That they all might be damned who believe not the truth, but had pleasure in unrighteousness."

The church of yesterday was divided over two separate beliefs in one man's teachings. The man was Moses. One side believed there was no such thing as angels nor spirits, and certainly no such thing as the resurrection of the dead, and in doing so, they completely ignored many Old Testament scriptures like (Psalm 69:28) where David prays, "Let them be blotted out of the book of the living, and not be written with the righteous." And (Exodus 32:32&33) where Moses said, 32 "Yet now, if thou wilt forgive their sin–; and if not, blot me, I pray thee, out of thy book which thou hast written. 33 And the Lord said unto Moses, Whosoever hath sinned against me, him will I blot out of my book."

I can understand, to some degree, ignoring the existence of the book of the living, if David or Moses, said that such a book exists. But when they read in their Tora, where Jehovah himself confirms the existence of the book of the living, by stating ("him will I blot out of my book"), they were without excuse! The other side believed there was such a thing as spirits and angels, and most definitely that there was such a thing as the resurrection of the dead!

The church today is also divided over two separate beliefs in one man's teachings; the apostle Paul. One side believes that if we continue in sin after we get saved, that the Lord will still accept us into the kingdom, because WORKs are not necessary. In doing so, they ignore many scriptures such as, (Matthew 7:21) in which Jesus himself stated, "Not every one that saith unto me, Lord, Lord, shall enter into the kingdom of heaven; but he that doeth the will of my father which is in heaven." And (John 9:4) where once again Jesus himself is speaking and it states, "I must work the works of him that sent me, while it is day: the night cometh, when no man can work." Or (Revelation 22:12) were also Jesus himself speaks and says, "And, behold, I come quickly; and my reward is with me, to give every man according as his work shall be." (Not according as his faith shall be!)

The other side believes that if we continue in sin after we get saved, that the Lord will not accept us into the kingdom.

We, just as the church of yesterday, have only one form of sound doctrine, the Bible. Only we have the whole Bible, whereas they had only half! Yet, we also have two separate beliefs. The reason for this is because we have one group of preachers and teachers who teach that we all sin and come short of the glory of God. As though we do it all the time and it is acceptable and no big thing. While on the other hand, we have preachers and teachers who teach that we all have sinned, and for that reason we all came short of the glory of God; meaning this is the reason we needed to get saved in the first place. Both of them cannot be correct! One is right and the other is wrong!

We have to read the word of God for ourselves to determine who is right and who is wrong. Read (Revelation 22:12) for yourself, without the help or the assistance of any other person on the earth. Then take pen and paper, then sit and think for as long as it takes for you to form your own opinion as to whether Jesus Christ himself (not the Apostle Paul, not your Pastor) is saying that all of mankind, yourself included, will be judged by their WORKS or is he saying they will be judged by their FAITH!

After you have formed your own opinion, take the pin and write down what your own opinion is. Never change what is written on the paper! You can then ask whoever you want to ask, as to what their opinion of what that scripture is saying. But always remember what you have written on the paper, even if you allow your Pastor or someone else to change your opinion, do not change what is written on the paper!

The only reason why I mentioned the Apostle Paul is because many of today's Theologians, Bishops, Doctors, Pastors, Preachers and teachers seem to think that they completely UNDERSTAND Paul's teachings. Now none of Paul's teachings are wrong, but many of his teachings are not easy to be understood. Mainly on the subject of FAITH and on the subject of WORKS. Some of his teachings are so difficult to understand, that even the Apostle Peter, who understood Paul's teachings better than any of today's top bible scholars, had this to say in (2nd Peter 3:15&16) 15"..........; even as our Beloved brother Paul also according to the wisdom given unto him hath written unto you; 16 As also in all his epistles, speaking in them of these things; in which are some things hard to be understood, which they that are unlearned and unstable wrest"(twist), "as they do also the other scriptures, unto their own destruction." In the book of (Romans 3: 23) it states, "For all have sinned, and come" (meaning came ,pass tense) "short of the glory of God;" You see, one of them is saying that we sin all the time, so don't worry about your sins, because the blood of Jesus automatically covers our sins, past, present and future.

In other words, they are teaching that you don't have to stop sinning in order to get to heaven, and that repentance is a nice thing to do, but it's not necessary. The other teaches that the blood of Christ only cleanses us of the sins we have already committed, sins of our past only. And even then, we have to first repent, which means stop doing it! There can be no forgiveness of sin unless repentance comes first! The Lord only forgives us for what we have done; not for what we are doing, nor for what we are going to do later on in life! In (Romans 3:25) it states, "Whom God have set forth to be a propitiation through faith in his blood, to declare his righteousness for the remission of sins that are past, through the forbearance of God;" The key word in this scripture is past, not present, not future, past only!

It is impossible to wash a pig completely clean from the top of its head to the bottom of its feet while it is still standing knee deep in the mud. The pig must first step out of the mud and then it can be completely cleansed. Likewise, we must step completely out of our sin before the blood of Christ can completely cleanse us *from head to toe. Repentance prepares us to be forgiven/cleansed. Repentance is God's way of simply saying to his children, who happen to be outside playing in the mud as children sometimes do, "Children, get out of that mud, so that I can give you a bath because it's almost dinner time!" There is no two ways about it, sin is mud and it spots whatever garment you are wearing!*

Before I quote these next scriptures I want to point out the fact that Jesus is directing this parable to those that are CALLED or what we commonly refer to as SAVED! In (Matthew 22:2&4&10-14) it states, 2 "The kingdom of heaven is like unto a certain king, which made a marriage for his son," 4 "Again he sent forth other servants, saying, Tell them which are bidden, Behold, I have prepared my dinner: my oxen and my fatlings are killed, and all things are ready: come unto the marriage." 10 "So those servants went out into the highways, and gathered together all as many as they found, both bad and good: and the wedding was furnished with guests. 11 And when the king came in to see the guests, he saw there a man which had not on a wedding garment: 12 and he saith unto him, Friend, how camest thou in hither not having a wedding garment? And he was speechless. 13 Then said the king to the servants, Bind him hand and foot, and take him away, and cast him into outer darkness; there shall be weeping and gnashing of teeth." (Well here comes the punch-line, or as some would say, the moral of the story.) 14 "For many are called, but few are chosen." This means many get saved, but few stay saved.

Many of us seem to think that God the Father's plan for the remission of man's sins began with his only begotten son Jesus Christ. But that is not so! God's plan was to first send John the Baptist so he could clear/prepare the way for Jesus to come and do his work. John was repentance, and Jesus was the actual remission of sin! First came repentance, and then came remission of sin. This is the order in which they came. John was even born before Jesus. Elisabeth, John's mother, was six months pregnant with John before the angel Gabriel even told Mary, Jesus's mother, that Elisabeth was six months pregnant; and to top that off, both John and Jesus were what we would call miracle births.

John's mother was too old to have a child, and Jesus's mother had never been with a man. But that's not all that was miraculous about John's birth. His birth was, and still is, the only documented case of reincarnation in the world! Why? Because Jesus himself said that John the Baptist was really Elias the prophet in the Greek tongue, but Elijah the prophet in the Hebrew tongue. The dictionary definition of the word reincarnation is this. Reincarnation is the religious or philosophical *concept that the soul or sprit, after biological death, begins a new life in a new body that may be human. Not only that, but both these two servants died, one behind the other in the order that they came. John was born first and carried out his part of the mission first, while Jesus waited for his time to begin his part of the mission, then John was assassinated. Jesus was born second, and carried out the remainder of that same mission, and then was also assassinated.*

These two were on a mission together for a reason; one without the other would be incomplete: thus remission of sin has to be accompanied by repentance or it is incomplete! Jesus himself could not say enough about the importance of John the Baptist, and the role he played in establishing the remission of sin, which in itself is the very definition of Salvation! God himself, initiated the New Covenant with Repentance, followed by Remission of Sin!

The third group of scriptures that provide answers as to why we have so many preachers and theologians in the world today, who teach that after a person is saved, he or she can continue on in sin and still go to heaven, can be found in (2nd Timothy 4:3&4) where Paul states, 3 "For the time will come when they will not endure sound doctrine; but after their own lust shall they heap to themselves teachers, having itching ears; 4. And they shall turn away their ears from the truth, and shall be turned unto fables." And in (2nd Peter 1:16) Peter stated, *"For we have not followed cunningly devised fables, when we made known unto you the power and coming of our Lord Jesus Christ, but were eyewitnesses of his majesty."* The dictionary definition of the word fable is (FICTION or a STORY). A prime example of a cunningly devised fable is when a preacher or teacher says *"a loving God would not cast his own children into a lake of fire just because they died in their sins."* The question I ask myself is, "Why did God send only one book into this world, the Bible, and why does that one book have only one topic, sin and its penalty, if your sins do not possess the power to disqualify you from being able to enter the kingdom of heaven?

Some will argue that the Bible does not speak only about sin and its penalty; it also speaks about righteousness and its reward. To that I say, yes this is true. But you have to ask yourself, what am I saying about the other side of the coin when I say that righteousness and reward is on this side of the coin. If I say heads is on this side of the coin, am I not also saying that tails is on the other side? Sin and its penalty on this side of the coin, and righteousness and its reward on the other side of the coin!

Chapter 7

The Role that Demonic Forces Play in Our Lives

Before I start, I just want to say that in order for mankind to fully understand him, we must fully understand what happened to Adam and Eve in the Garden of Eden! When the devil entered into the serpent. We start there because there were three bodies that the devil used to get to where he is today. He used the snake basically because the snake was at the top of the food chain when it comes to the lower forms of life, plus the snake could also talk.

In the first part of Genesis 3:1 it states, "Now the serpent was more subtle than any beast of the field which the Lord had made……." (The word subtle means smart.) Genesis 2:9 states, "And out of the ground made the Lord God to grow every tree that is pleasant to the sight, and good for food; the tree of life also in the midst of the garden, and the tree of knowledge of good and evil."

Genesis 2:16&17 states, 16 "And the Lord God commanded the man, saying, of every tree of the garden thou mayest freely eat: 17 But of the tree of the knowledge of good and evil, thou shalt not eat of it: for in the day that thou eatest thereof thou shalt surely die."

As I said before, the devil used three bodies in to achieve his goal, which was to dwell on the inside of the bodies of mankind forever, if everything went according to his plan. So he started with the snake. No one knows how he managed to get inside the snake, but it is clearly evident that the snake disobeyed the Lord in some way that resulted in the devil being able to get on the inside of it. Another reason why I say the snake obviously disobeyed is because when the Lord issued each one of them their punishment, he started with the snake and then proceeded to the woman and finally the man; and since the man and woman's punishment was due to disobedience, we can only assume the snake's punishment was also due to disobedience. I used the word assume because the scripture says that I can only teach what I know. In 1st Corinthians 13:9 it states, "For we know in part, and we prophesy in part."

Before I go any further I would like to say this, there are many scholars and teachers in the world today who teach that the serpent in the book of Genesis was literally the devil. Nothing could be further from the truth. Take the time to examine the scripture, especially the part where the Lord announced the punishment for the serpent for its part in causing Adam and Eve to bite from the tree of the knowledge of good and evil.

Genesis 3:14&15 states, 14"And the Lord God said unto the serpent, Because thou hast done this, thou art cursed above all cattle, and above every beast in the field; upon thy belly shalt thou go," (The devil does not crawl on his belly.) "And dust shalt thou eat all the days of thy life:" (The devil does not eat dust, but snakes do because they eat their prey right off the ground.) 15 "And I will put enmity between thee and the woman, and between thy seed and her seed; it shall bruise thy head, and thou shalt bruise his heel."

First, the devil has no means of reproduction! Ever since that day snakes have always been considered an enemy to mankind and mankind an enemy to snakes! A snake will either bite mankind or run from them, and mankind will either find something to smash a snake's head or run from the snake.

I said all that to say this; the devil is the enemy of God, and we are the offspring of God, so the devil was already the enemy of mankind before Adam and Eve bit the fruit of the tree of the knowledge of good and evil. The serpent was not an enemy to mankind in the beginning because Eve would not have been having a conversation with the serpent had it been an enemy. Had it been an enemy at that time, Eve would have run from it, instead of having a conversation with it! The devil entered into the snake, then used the snake's vocal cords to talk Eve into biting off of the tree. Then when Eve bit the fruit of the tree of the knowledge of good and evil, the devil entered into Eve, and then used Eve to persuade Adam to bite. When he bit the fruit, the devil entered into Adam also!

In the beginning Adam was the only one living inside Adam's body. When God the Father and God the Son created Eve, Eve was the only one living inside Eve's body. But at the moment they ate of the fruit of the tree of the knowledge of good and evil, they both received two more spirits. Inside Adam's body there was Adam plus what is called an unclean spirit, plus what is called a clean spirit. Three spirits living inside Adam's one body, Adam included, because Adam himself was a spirit, living in his own body. Three spirits living inside Eve's body, Eve included, because Eve herself was a spirit, living inside her own body, which is called a *temple. After they bit of the tree, three spirits living in one body became what I call the new internal spiritual molecular structure of all mankind. Before they ate of the tree, the internal spiritual molecular structure of mankind consisted of only one spirit per body, or you could say one spirit per temple.*

Before I go any further, I feel the need to say this; If we can somehow arrive at the understanding that our body is a temporary part of us, it belongs to us, but it is not us. If we can arrive at this understanding, then we will have reached a point where this sample of life has finally begun to make sense. In order for us to stay alive in the world that we now live in, we must stay inside this body. When looking at it from this point of view, it seems like the body is some kind of space suit that we must wear while on this strange planet. This concept of the body is helpful to those who think their body is indeed who they are. I say that it is a helpful concept because it brings a person's understanding closer to whom and what they really are.

But when we come into the knowledge of just how many spirits one body is capable of accommodating, then it is time to embrace yet another even deeper concept, which is Jesus's concept of what your body really is, and that is this; your body is really and truly a temple, designed to house your spirit and Jesus's spirit.

In (1st Corinthians 6:13) it states, "Meats for the belly, and the belly for meats: but God shall destroy both it and them. Now the body is not for fornication, but for the Lord; and the Lord for the body." In Mark 5:13 Jesus cast about 2,000 unclean spirits out of one man, just to give you an idea of how many unclean spirits one body can accommodate! "And forthwith Jesus gave them leave, And the unclean spirits went out, and entered into the swine: and the herd ran violently down a steep place into the sea, (they were about two thousand:) and were choked in the sea."

Now back to what I was saying. The clean spirit is literally the knowledge of good, and the unclean spirit is literally the knowledge of evil. Genesis 3:10&11 states, "10 and he said, I heard thy voice in the garden, and I was afraid, because I was naked; and I hid myself. 11 And he said, WHO TOLD THEE that thou was naked? Hast thou eaten of the tree, where of I commanded thee that thou shouldest not eat?"

Verse 11 is where the Lord himself asked two questions, yet in his two questions he reveals three extremely vital pieces of information. In his second question he reveals the only possible location their new knowledge could have come from, which was the tree of the knowledge of good and evil. However, it was in his first question that the two most vital pieces of information were revealed to mankind! I say this, because without this information it is virtually impossible for mankind to even begin to understand the ongoing turmoil within themselves; mainly the continuous inability to experience victory over committing the act of sin! In his first question he did not ask Adam and Eve, "How did you find out you where naked?" Nor did he ask them, "What brought you to the conclusion that you were naked?" Instead, he used the word WHO!

Now I am sure there are some who, in their effort to explain away the truth, will offer God some of their expert assistance in selecting a better word vocabulary. But I for one do not consider God to be mentally incompetent at all! So when the Good Lord asked them who, he meant just that, WHO? Now the revelation in the word "who" is the fact that it refers to only two entities, either a being or a human being. The Good Lord used the word "who" because he and his Son created the Garden of Eden and everything and everyone in it. Although the serpent could talk, it is still considered a thing, not a who. He knew that there were only two human beings in the garden, and they did not have that kind of knowledge. He also knew there were intelligent beings in the garden, and that they did have that kind of knowledge, but they were confined to the tree of the knowledge of good and evil.

The next word the Lord used to give revelation to us at this day in time, is the word TOLD. The word "told" is past tense to the word "tell" and the word tell is directly related to the word TALK. Since we are referring to past tense, then the word would have to be TALKED, and so when you put the two main words together, the revelation that appears is "Being Talked"! The best definition of the word "being" would be, existence, whether visible or invisible, and also, whether good or evil. A ghost is a being that is invisible to everyone, except to the person whom the ghost appears to. The second half of Exodus 3:14 states, "and he said, Thus shalt thou say unto the children of Israel, I AM hath sent me unto you." In this verse, the words I AM only mean I Exist, yet they insinuate, (whether visible or not!)

Now the reason why I quoted the second half of Exodus 3:14 is because in it, God himself stresses the fact that he is present and he is real, which leads me to stress the fact that the enemies of both us and our God are real and exist, only closer, much-much closer than most of us ever imagined!

I heard it said before, that the devil's greatest accomplishment was convincing men that he does not exist. I am sorry to say it, but I have to disagree. The reason is because less than 10 percent of the world's population believes that there is no devil. Less than 10 percent does not constitute the title greatest accomplishment. However, he has achieved an accomplishment that possibly more than 95 percent of the world's population is unaware of and it alone is no doubt, his most effective weapon!

The tree of knowledge of good and evil. First of all, let us elaborate on exactly what the first half of that tree's name or title means. Knowledge of good, biblically speaking, translates directly to the meaning clean spirit. These spirits are guiding spirits, and they come from God.

Now all of this talk about beings and their direct relation to the word knowledge is geared to place your mind in an ideal atmosphere, conducive to fully understanding the first half of Genesis 3:22, "And the Lord God said, Behold, the man is become as one of us, to know good and evil:... " This statement means that one being, which is Adam, has allowed two beings to enter into him, one good and one evil, causing man to become similar to God himself. I used the word similar because it is the best word to describe mankind's newly developed thought process (at least it was new at the time.)

There is a difference between the way Adam and Eve thought before they bit of the tree and the way they thought after they bit of the tree. Before the tree, the only voices Adam or Eve ever heard were each other's voice, God's voice, the snake's voice and their own internal voice. An accurate description of one's own internal voice would be to count to ten, in your head, or to repeat instructions given to you, so as not to forget, also in your head. When we do this, we hear the numbers or the words, on the inside of our mind.

But after they bit of the tree, Adam and Eve were totally unaware of the fact that they were hearing voices they never heard before! They did, however, recognize that they seemed to have more new ideas. The verse that reveals this is a statement in the middle of Genesis 3:6, where it starts with, "And when the woman saw that the tree was…. And... and a tree to be desired to make one wise, ……"

I skipped through the verse because I only want to focus on what Adam and Eve perceived to be an improved way of thinking. You see, what Adam and Eve considered to be a new way of thinking and nothing more, God called it listening to voices and nothing more! Adam did not tell God that anyone told him anything, let alone the fact that he was naked. As a matter of fact, Adam's main concern was to avoid the embarrassment of being seen undressed; while at the same time, not noticing the fact that he didn't even know what being naked meant the day before.

Mankind used to use pictures in caves, in order to say words. Now we use words to paint a picture in each other's mind of what it is we are trying to get each other to see. That is exactly what I am trying to do here. Something took place in the Garden of Eden that I can see clearly because the Holy Spirit himself showed it to me. For me to show it to you, I have to paint you a picture using words. So it would be good for you to try to get to a place where you are not likely to be distracted. Why? Because the dark rulers of this world have been able to conceal, not only their own identity and their location, but also their method of operation. I will be explaining exactly how it is that they do what they do, inside each and every one of us day in, day out, year in, year out, for approximately the past 6,000 years! All because we, like Adam, did not fully understand what happened in the garden. But the time has come in which the lord has decided that we should finally understand.

I am going to give you an example of what happened in the garden, but this example is designed hopefully, to only cause you to begin to understand. If you think you understand after hearing the example, then your mind is already preparing to take you down the wrong track, because the Lord has only allowed me to put into this example enough to cause you to begin to understand.

Imagine this; a man and a woman raise a little girl at home until she is six years old. They know everything that she knows, because she is their only child and they taught her everything she knows. This is called home schooling. So the mother and father decide to go out to dinner and for the first time they get a babysitter to watch their daughter. So everything works out according to plan, they have dinner, dance and then come home. They pay the babysitter and take her home.

So the next morning at the breakfast table while in the middle of their meal, the little girl says to her father, "Daddy, when do you think my ministration period will start?"

Well the mother and father both look at each other, and turn purple in the face! When they regained their composure, the first three words that came out of their mouth is #1 **Who** #2 **Told** #3 **You!** *Because the mother and father knew for sure that neither of them told the child this. So their next question was obvious.* **"Did you talk to the babysitter?"**

Now in a way, this is exactly what happened in the garden. (Genesis 3:11) The parent of Adam and Eve went away for just a little while and when he returned, his children knew something they were not supposed to know. So his first three words were #1 **Who** #2 **Told** #3

You! *So God's next question was also obvious,* **"Did You eat of the tree?"** *Remember, I did not say that the example was exactly what happened in the garden, I said it was exactly like it, in a way!*

This is only, what I call a surface level understanding. As we go deeper you will see more and more, the deeper we go. I say that because what took place on the surface was a change you can see with the spiritual eye and hear with the spiritual ear, not only you the reader, but Adam and Eve, both were at least aware of an internal change that gave them what seemed to be a better perception of their external surroundings. Ninety-five percent of you, the readers, will instantly understand my next statement by experience. Five percent will form an understanding, based upon observation. What I am going to say is not an example; it is literal, even though it could easily be mistaken as an example. Adam and Eve did back then, what we do today; we become compelled by either our so-called own curiosity, or by another person, to try alcohol, which is derived from a plant; marijuana, which is a plant; or cocaine in any form, especially crack! Which is derived from a plant. And finally heroin in any form, which also comes from a plant.

I realize that we might do it initially for the medical reasons, but that does not stop a person from mildly to severely experiencing the same experience as the per-

son using it for recreational reasons. We use any one of these plants or substances derived from plants, because it seemingly temporarily enhances some aspect of the life we live. We think differently while under the influence of whatever mood altering substance we put in our body. Some think they can do this particular thing better, and others think they can do that particular thing better. In many cases it is true, because different drugs do indeed cause different people to be able to do different things better. The problem is this; we are not aware of the reality, that as we take these mind altering substances into our body/temple in excess, we also, simultaneously open up what is referred to as a window, whereby unclean spirits enter into your temple/body.

The reason they are called windows instead of doors is because only a clean spirit can enter into your temple by way of the door. The unclean spirits have no key to a house in which the Lord built for himself to live in; so for them to enter, they do what thieves do. They wait for one of the windows of your temple to be opened and they break in. To be even more specific, they wait for the unclean spirit that already lives inside our temple to persuade us to take a drug or drink alcohol in excess, thereby opening up a window, which in turn they use to break in.

Remember, we are all born with both a clean and an unclean spirit inside, not inside us, but inside the body that we live in. It is that unclean spirit which persuades us to open windows in our own temples. John 10:1&2 states, 1 "Verily, verily, I say unto you, He that entereth not by the door into the sheepfold, but climbeth up some other way, the same is a thief and a robber. 2 But he that entereth in by the door is the shepherd of the sheep." I mentioned earlier that we today are doing the same thing Adam and Eve did in the garden. So I would suppose that you would like to know in what way?

Well the answer is this; we notice the psychological effect, as well as the possible physical sensation that accompanies the excessive use of whatever alcohol or drug we choose to use. But we, like Adam and Eve, are totally oblivious to the undisputable fact that as we do so, we allow an undetermined number of demonic unclean spirits to enter into our temple. The more we repeat the activity, the more we take on more and more unclean spirits. Then one day when we decide to stop the activity all together, to our surprise we find out we cannot stop. This is known as what is called, a Strong-Hold. Strong-hold is just another word for Demonic Possession, which can range from mild to severe. Today's modern scientific world refers to it as addiction, and they deny any allegations of demonic presence.

Now Adam and Eve did not deny the presence of demonic spirits, nor did they concede, they were simply unaware, just as 95% of the world's population today is unaware.

Before I go any further, let's go back closer to the beginning. There is more than one reason as to why the Lord God put a good spirit inside the tree along with the evil spirit. One reason was because he knew what an evil spirit was capable of, and he knew that no man nor woman would stand a chance if they were to accidently, or intentionally, touch the tree, and the evil spirit were to enter into them without the benefit of the good spirit simultaneously entering into them also. He knew they would become slaves to evil unclean spirits instantly! In (1st Corinthians 10:13) it states, "There hath no temptation taken you but such as is common to man: but God is faithful, who will not suffer you to be tempted above that ye are able; but will with the temptation also make a way to escape, that ye may be able to bare it.,"

This is exactly what the lord God did in the Garden of Eden. The evil spirit/knowledge of evil is The Voice of Evil, and it tempts us. While at the same time, the good spirit/knowledge of good, makes a way for us to escape the temptation, which is in turn what I call The Voice of Reason. The voice of reason speaks to us during our moment of temptation and advises us on how to escape the tremendous gravitational pull of temptation.

The voice of reason works in many ways. The voice knows how weak and how strong we are. Two of the ways it works is: 1. If we are too weak to endure a particular temptation, it advises us to avoid it. 2. If we are strong enough to endure a particular temptation, it guides us through it. The voice speaks before, during and after every temptation. I would be tempted to say that all human beings engage in conversation with it all the time, while being unaware that it exists. We call it talking to ourselves when we do it audibly, and thinking to ourselves when do it using only our internal voice. Note: (talk=communicate and communication cannot take place unless at least two entities are involved.) By the way, 99% of the world's population mistakenly refers to the knowledge of good as their Conscience! Believe it or not the dictionary even has it incorrect to some small degree. The normal dictionary definition of the word conscience is "An inner feeling or voice viewed as acting as a guide to the rightness or wrongness of one's behavior." This is an accurate description of the spirit that lives in all of us .

The Bible concordance dictionary definition is not entirely correct, yet it is more to the point. The concordance definition is, "to understand, or become aware of, or know.", which is what took place in the garden of Eden.

Although many of us read the Bible on a regular basis, we are still largely unaware of the plan the devil had for our lives. The devil, from the beginning, had a plan which included four steps. If he could succeed in achieving all four steps, then he would have accomplished what was at the time his overall goal. I say (what was at the time, his overall goal) because the devil's purpose towards man has not always been to kill, steal and destroy. What? Yes, it is true. Why? Because there was a point in time when the devil's purpose towards man was a fate that is difficult to imagine; a fate in which all hope of man ever being reconciled unto God our Father would be destroyed. Control of the temple we now live in, called the body, would be stolen forever! Thus his initial purpose toward man was to steal and destroy. Killing us entered the picture only after he realized God was five steps ahead of him and was not going to allow him to carry out his original master plan.

When the devil and one third of the angels were kicked out of heaven, they were immediately faced with a number of problems. Number one was the fact that they were all going to be thrown into the lake of fire if they could not figure out a way to avoid it. Number two was the extremely uncomfortable reality, that they *literally only had somewhere in the neighborhood of approximately seven days before they would be cast into the lake of fire. If they could solve the number one problem, the number two problem would solve itself. Now these approximate seven days were days according to God's time, which is a thousand years of man's time = one day of God's time. I call it God's time, but there is a name for it, and that name is called eternity.*

Contrary to popular belief, eternity is not a place where time does not exist. Instead, eternity is a place where time does exist, it's just that from man's point of view, it appears that they took a 24-hour day and stretched it to make it last 1,000 years, and instead of limiting how much time we get, they made it unlimited. But I'll tell you something that is funny; from the angel's point of view it is right the opposite. The way they see it, God took a 1,000 year day, and shrunk it to make it last only 24 hours in our world, not their world and then put a limit on how many of those shrunken days you get. These are two different views, yet both are correct in their own respect. Proof?

God lives in eternity, where the paradise of God is located. There are two paradises; one is located in heaven above and the other is located beneath those of us who live on the earth. Revelation 2:7 states, "He that hath an ear, let him hear what the spirit saith unto the churches; To him that overcometh will I give to eat of the tree of life, which is in the midst of the paradise of God." (This confirms that one paradise is up in heaven where both God and the tree of life is located, and the other paradise is downward where Jesus told the man, "Today you will be with me in paradise".)

Revelation 22:2 states, "In the midst of the street of it, and on either side of the river, was there the tree of life, which bare twelve manner of fruits, and yielded her fruit every month: and the leaves of the tree were for the healing of the nations." (This confirms that time does exist where God is located, because where there is no time, there is no measure of time, and where there is time, of course, there is a measure of time. Time is measured in increments such as, seconds, minutes, hours, days, weeks, months, years and so on! This verse confirms that months exist where God is located and if months exist there, then so do weeks and hours and so on!)

That being said, I will return to the four-step master plan the devil implemented to avoid being cast into the lake of fire ever, let-alone in approximately seven days. His first step was to enter the snake. That worked out well. Before I get into these steps any further, I would like address the person who does not believe animals can, nor ever could, talk. Find a talking black bird or *parakeet and tell it that it is not true, and that it is just a silly childish fairy tale. Oh, and don't let anyone see you talking to a snake-I-mean-bird!*

His second step was to use the snake's ability to talk in order to talk the woman into eating from the tree, so that he could go before her, re-enter the tree, and enter the woman. That worked out well also. His third step was to use the woman to persuade the man to eat of the tree so that one of his demons could enter into the man. That also worked out just fine. His fourth and final step, now that he and his demons were in both the man and the woman was to persuade both to eat of the Tree of Life so that they would live forever, trapped inside their own (body/temple.)

You see, the only way for a man to re-enter heaven, which is where we all come from, is to leave the body behind. In (1stCorinthian 15:50) it states, "Now this I say, brethren, that flesh and blood cannot inherit the kingdom of God;……" Which means we have to be able to die! The inside of Adam and Eve had become the first two new(homes) or (places to dwell in) for the devil and one or more of his demons, even though Adam and Eve both were unaware of it. In the first half of Matthew 12:44, Jesus said demons refer to a human's body as their own (house), and in Romans 7:20, Paul said that, he himself is not totally responsible for him doing some of the bad things he's done in his lifetime. He says there is a demon that (dwells inside him) that tries to compels him to do bad things, whether he does them or not!

Matthew 12:43 & half of 44 states, 43 "When the unclean spirit is gone out of a man, he walketh through dry places, seeking rest, and findeth none. 44 Then he saith, I will return into my house from whence I came out;... ... ... " I underlined the words I and my, in order to emphasize exactly how possessive minded these demons are, over a human body that doesn't even belong to him or them, whatever the case may be. Question? Have you ever loaned something of yours to someone, and they kept it so long that they began to think and act like it was theirs? Well that is the case with the unclean spirits that Jesus is talking about in Matthew 12:43&44. These unclean spirits have lived inside the same body that we live in for so long, that they refer to it as their house.

Another point I would like to bring out is the fact that they refer to it as a house, and we refer to it as our body. We are both correct, but they are more correct.

If we begin to refer to our body as our house, then we will be closer to operating on the level of understanding they are operating on, because they are operating on a MUCH-MUCH higher level of understanding than we are. Romans 7:20 states, "Now if I do that I would not, it is no more I that do it, but sin that dwelleth in me." (An unclean spirit itself is nothing but sin.) Adam and Eve were unaware of the demonic presence inside them, but the clean spirit, which was also dwelling inside them, in his effort to alert God to the fact that he was present inside Adam, compelled Adam to say to God that he was naked; knowing all along that as soon as the Lord heard Adam say that he was naked, he would immediately know the clean spirit was inside him. If the clean spirit was in him, so was the unclean spirit also, and if a un-unclean spirit was in him, then his next move would be to compel them both to eat of the Tree of Life, and live forever. The unclean spirits kept quiet hoping to not be detected!

Now the Lord already knew what Adam had done, but he allowed the clean spirit to perform his responsibility, which was to compel Adam to do the right thing before, during and after any sin he might commit.

There was no problem with mankind living forever before the unclean spirits entered into them. But after the unclean spirits entered into mankind, to allow mankind to eat of the tree of life, would have been an everlasting disaster. The reason I say that is because every human being is now born with an unclean, and a clean spirit inside our bodies, plus we ourselves, so that makes a minimum of three spirits in one body. The only way for our spirit/us to be rejoined with our Father in heaven, is for the body we live in to die! (Correction: we as human beings do not have a spirit, we are a spirit.) If the Lord would have allowed Adam and Eve to continue to live within reach of the tree of life, then the devil and his demons would have compelled them both to eat of the tree of life. If that would have happened, the human body would not be able to die, which would have made the human body an everlasting house for the demonic spirits to live in, and thereby solving the number one problem for the devil and his demons. They will have successfully figured out how to avoid ever being thrown into the lake of fire.

Not only that, mankind struggles today in a battle between good and evil. Imagine a world in which all of the powerful evil men who ever lived were still evil, still powerful and still alive. Imagine a world in which there were 50 times more humans walking the earth, than there are now. Imagine a world in which the good, clean spirit that is in us now, could only lead us around in this world, because it could never lead us home to God the Father.

Jesus Christ is indeed the Savior of the world, but when he died on the cross that was not the first time he and the Father has saved us. They saved us from the very beginning, in the garden.

Earlier I mentioned that there was a number one and a number two problem that the devil and his angels were facing immediately after being kicked out of heaven. When the Lord separated Adam and Eve from the Tree of Life, that eliminated all possibilities of the devil and his fallen angels being able to avoid being thrown into the lake of fire. Genesis 3:22-24 states, 22 "And the lord God said, Behold, the man is become as one of us, To know good and evil: and now, lest he put forth his hand, and take also of the tree of life, and eat and live forever: 23. Therefore the Lord God sent him forth from the Garden of Eden, to till the ground from whence he was taken. 24. So he drove out the man; and he placed at the east of the garden of Eden Cherubims, and a flaming sword which turned every way, to keep the way of the tree of life." (Keeping the way of the tree of life means to preserve its intended purpose, which was to bless mankind.)

So that left the devil and his angles to face there number two problem. But before I go into the number two problem, I need to be sure that we are on the same page. The devil's first attempt was to convert the bodies of mankind into permanent housing for him and his fallen angels by the billions, by way of what we call natural childbirth. Now his number two problem had turned out to be the only one that he was going to be able to do anything about.

This problem is a little difficult to explain, and even more difficult to understand; mainly because it involves two kinds of pressure. Time! Time alone relieves pressure when you have plenty of it, plenty of time to think, plenty of time to plan a course of action. But when you do not have anywhere near the amount of time you need to resolve a life-threatening situation, then the small, inefficient amount of time that you do have automatically converts itself into raw pressure, which increases in its intensity as each moment slips away.

It is kind of like a mother who has a child who has fallen into a hole, and the child has only 10 minutes to live unless someone can get to the child. The problem is the fact that it is going to take at least 45 minutes to get to the child. This is what is called mental anguish. I am using words to try to paint a picture of the mental state this mother would be in. To get the clearest picture of what it would feel like mentally, you have to imagine yourself in the place of that mother, and meditate on it a while. You see in this scenario, the shortage of time has sealed the fate of the child!

Another more-to-the-point example. Imagine you accidentally killed a person in a car accident, and the judge sentenced you to be burned alive unto death in exactly seven days. This would produce tremendous pressure and mental anguish. In the second half of

(Revelation 12:12) it states, "Woe to the inhibiters of the earth and of the sea! for the devil is come down unto you, having great wrath, because he knoweth that he hath but a short time."

From Adam to Jesus was approximately 4,000 years, and from Jesus to right now is a little over 2,000 years. Together that comes to a little over 6,000 years. According to the events accruing in the world today, we are living in the last day, not the last days. In other words, the last 1,000 years. So when you take into account the fact that 1,000 man-years equal one day, not only to God, but also to anyone living in the spiritual realm, it means that mankind has entered into the day in which the Lord will return. In other words, we have entered the seventh day. Seven days is not what mankind would call a long time, but it does meet the criteria to be viewed as a short time as mentioned in Revelation 12:12. As far as man is concerned, by our time, the devil has been in this world for a little over 6,000 years; not exactly what we would call a short time by man's standard.

But by time according to an angel 6,000 years is only six very short days. The devil and all of his demons are angels. So in their minds they only had about 7 days before they would be cast into the lake of fire. Now do you understand what I mean when I say, the mental anguish of not having enough time to think of what to do to avoid being thrown into a lake of fire; there simply wasn't much time! This is why Revelation 12:12 says, "he hath but a short time." By entering into the body of man, 7 days transformed into 7,000 years inside mind of the devil and his demons. Of course this was only while inside a human body. Talk about taking a chill-pill!

Now aside from the mental anguish that the shortage of time presented, there was another factor added to the equation. This was the fact that they had no access to water, and possibly no food either. I say possibly no food because it seems fitting, but I have found no scripture to confirm my assumption. Matthew 12:43 states, "When the unclean spirit is gone out of a man, he walketh through dry places, seeking rest and findeth none." When unclean spirits are not inside a man, woman or child, they suffer a tremendous thirst.

Also if a man be a non-believer, and he becomes converted into a unclean spirit; he himself will suffer a similar fate at the point of his death! But if a man is a believer, and he becomes converted into an unclean spirit, then instead of meeting such a fate at the point of death, he will meet the same fate on judgment day in the lake of fire. Luke 16:23&24 states, 23 "And in hell he lifted up his eyes, being in torments, and seeth Abraham afar off, and Lazarus in his bosom 24 And he cried and said, Father Abraham, have mercy on me, and send Lazarus, that he may dip the tip of his finger in water, and cool my tongue; for I am tormented in this flame."

I can remember some time ago when I was homeless and desperate, and had spent all that I had on foolishness, like the prodigal son. I had gone, I think , about two days without water or food. As I was walking down the street, I became a little fearful that my level of dehydration was getting to a dangerous point. My tongue stuck to the roof of my mouth and it was about 95 degrees outside. I couldn't swallow because I had no spit. I saw a person sitting on their porch, and I swallowed what little pride I had and I asked in a most humble way, for a glass of water. They gave me a good cold glass of ice water and it relieved my suffering. I never forgot that feeling. The point I am trying to bring out is this, even though I was desperately suffering, there was no-way-in- the-world that I was going to waste my request for water, by asking for a single drop off of someone's fingertip. I think that the Lord has blessed me with an exceptional imagination, but even so, I cannot wrap my mind around the concept of being in such destitute state of suffering, that I would make such a request!

I made mention earlier, about being converted into an unclean spirit. That is really what this whole life is about; being converted into either a clean spirit or into an unclean spirit. In Luke 16:24, we are looking at a situation in which the rich man had been successfully converted into an unclean spirit, and the poor man was successfully converted into a clean spirit!

In a way, I really wish there was a softer way to say this, but the truth is most of the world was, and is, under the grand delusion that when we get to heaven, God is going to convert us, or reprogram our minds to do the right thing at all times. All of us will undergo conversion, but not in heaven. It is happening here on the earth as we eat, sleep and breathe. But mostly as we think and respond to what appears to be our own thoughts.

(While I am on the subject of thoughts that appear to be our own, let me just say this. When human beings attempt to utilize one of the most powerful and most precious gifts that the Lord has given to all his children, the unclean spirits go to work on persuading us that the gift does not work. The gift is the gift of faith. They derail your train of thought by replacing it with their own train of thought! The reason why they attack a Christian who is making an attempt to try to learn how to use their faith is because without faith it is impossi-

ble to please God. Faith can do anything, and the demonic unclean spirits fear it more than anything on the earth.)

The method that they use is, they throw thoughts before your mind, both verbal and visual, in an effort to change the channel that your mind is on. In other words, when a Christian man looks at a woman walking in front of him, and his mind starts to try to lust after her, he recognizes what is about to happen in his mind. So he looks the other way, or he channels his thinking to a good thought and keeps it there until his mind fully embraces the good thought. Then later he may ask himself where in the world did that thought come from? The answer is: it came from the unclean spirit or spirits that dwell inside your body with you. It or they tossed the thought before your imagination in an effort to activate your imagination to the intent of gaining your approval to go ahead and relish in the lustful thought.

Now the main question is, why do they seek your approval? And the answer is
#1. They enjoy it just as much as you do, if not more.
#2. They cannot do it without your approval! You see, the instant you agree to relish in the lustful thought, is also the instant that you believed, and claimed the thought itself as though it were your very own thought. In reality, the thought itself did not origi-

nate in your mind at all. It originated in the mind of the unclean spirit and all you did was co-sign it. Then you and the unclean spirits within you went ahead and enjoyed yourselves lusting. But had you never claimed it, then the thought would have ended without ever fully manifesting in your mind. Alt-hough you can bet your life that the enemy within you will make more than one or two attempts to get you to claim that thought!

Now I said all that to say this. When it comes to faith, the unclean spirits work the exact same way. The only difference is they try a whole lot harder to get you to claim the thoughts they throw at you. For example, you may be in need of a car to get to work and take the kids to doctor appointments and things like that. But you have saved $1,500 to try to pay cash for an older model car, because you really can't afford to pay monthly payments. So you pray to the Lord and ask him to lead you to a good car that you can get for cash. You begin praying and waiting on the Lord to send you the right car; but its two weeks later and nothing has happened. Then thoughts start to bombard your mind saying, "What if the Lord says no." Or what if this, or what if that. Then thoughts of making a down payment on a new car with monthly payments begin attacking you. The unclean spirit cannot stop your faith. So he uses thoughts opposite of your thoughts in an effort to convince you that your faith gift from God just doesn't work, there's something wrong with it and it's broken. When in reality, there's nothing wrong with it, it's just fine and works every time. It's just that you allow him to talk you into using it against yourself. Because you get what you believe you will get instead of what you want every time. You are convinced these thoughts that control your faith are yours! You see it appeared to be Adam's thought that he was naked. But God said that some being told him he was naked.

From the day we are born, both the clean and unclean spirit inside the body we are born in begins the process of attempting to convert us into what they are. From the beginning, we are neither a clean spirit, nor are we a unclean spirit. We are simply an innocent spirit. I was amazed when the Lord revealed to me how soon the unclean spirit begins to go to work on the innocent spirit.

Question! Have you ever had the opportunity to babysit a child so young that they had not yet learned how to walk? You may have had to spank the baby a time or two for playing with electric sockets in the hallway. So let us say you are in the living room and you are watching television while keeping an eye on the baby. The baby is playing with the toys, but he or she is also looking up at you every now-and-then to see if you are looking at him or are you looking at the television. When he looks at you, and sees you are looking at him, he keeps on playing with the toy. But when he sees that you are looking at the television, he takes off crawling fast as he can, trying to make it to that electric socket.

Many would look at this scenario and say, (well, it is only natural for little toddlers to do things like that.) But those of us who say that are incorrect. As grownups and as adolescents, we always check to make sure no one is watching us when we are getting ready to do something wrong. Now the question is, Is this natural or normal behavior for adults and adolescents in the civilized world we live in today, or is there something more sinister at work?

The answer is there is definitely something more sinister at work. Now when we as grownups or adolescents indulge in this devious behavior, whether we do it all the time or once every so-often, the chances are it is not our first, second, third, fourth or fiftieth time. The point is this, if we, as grownups and adolescents, are willing to admit that when we indulge in devious behavior, something sinister is at work, whether it be our thirtieth or our fortieth time doing it, then why do we have a hard time admitting something sinister was at work the first time we did it. Which is my point exactly.

You see this little child is so young that he does not know how to use the restroom, does not know how to walk and hasn't even said mama yet, so you know that he doesn't know how to talk yet. However, look at what this child is able to perform for the very first time. He is able to cleverly out maneuver the parent or the baby sitter. Not only is it a devious act, but it is also an act of disobedience. The subject is too young to receive instruction from any outside source, and since the act itself was an act of disobedience, we know the child was not being instructed by the knowledge of good/clean spirit. That leaves only one other source, the knowledge of evil/unclean spirit! The child is being communicated with in the tongues of angels/spirits, which we all know, because we ourselves are all spirits, but we do not yet know that we know.

In (1st Corinthians 14:2) it states, "For he that speaketh in an unknown tongue speaketh not unto men, but unto God: for no man understandeth him; howbeit in the spirit he speaketh mysteries." This scripture is referring to the language we all know, but do not know that we know! The language of spirits/angels is the same whether clean or unclean.

The Lord has taken me behind enemy lines to give the church a good look at exactly how the enemy operates. Why me? I do not know! The clean spirit speaks as well, but most of the benefits of obeying the clean spirit are long term, compared to the seemingly instant benefits advertised by the unclean spirit. Almost every desire we experience has two ways of being obtained, the quick way or the slow way, at least that is how it is perceived in a little child's mind. In reality, it is a matter of the wrong/quick way or the right/slow way. This is how life is perceived to 90% of the world's grownups! So a little toddler is seriously out matched. I do not blame mothers, but the Lord has designed the mother to better understand young children.

We can no longer wait until children become 12 and 13 years old before we decide to get serious about teaching a child about the Lord. By the time a child is 12 years old, she or he has had 11 years of internal unclean upbringing. There are qualities in parents that a child eventually pick up on, but a child should not be left to pick up on the things that a parent can easily install into a child if you start at an early age. We are instructed by the Lord to fight for our children from the very beginning. Proverbs 22:6 states, "Train up a child in the way he should go: and when he is old, he will not depart from it." When a dog is 12 years old you do not decide to take it out to show it some new tricks. You start when it is a puppy! A wise teacher knows this. Our enemy is a wise teacher! If preparing your child for this world is your first priority, then when the child grows up and has *children of its own, preparing his or her children for this world also will be his or her first priority. But if preparing your child for the world to come is your first priority, then when your child has children of their own, preparing them for the world to come will also be their first priority!*

I am going to elaborate on the unclean spirit for a while because he is the one we know the least about, and he is the one doing all the damage. His presence inside us has been kept secret in the worst way for a little over 6,000 years. Their presence inside us operates a little like getting someone to help you find the person who stole your money, but what you don't know is that the one you chose to help you find the thief, is the thief. So you and he, together, will never find the thief!

Let's start with what we refer to as thinking. In the example I gave earlier with the young toddler, I said the child was being communicated with. This is the way that it works. The unclean being says to the child, "I'm going to cry for my bottle of milk." instead of saying to the child, "You cry for your bottle of milk." The child heard the words of the unclean spirit and considered the words he heard to be his own thought. Because the spirit did not use second person communication terminology. Instead, he used self-communication terminology.

The unclean spirit is, in a sense, a parasite, and the child's mind and body is the host. The objective of the parasite/unclean spirit is to never allow the host to become aware that he is present. Also to keep the child convinced for the rest of its life that the voice he hears during the so-called process of thinking is the child's own mind's voice and words. Adolescent's own mind's voice and words. Young adult's own mind's voice and words. Senior citizen's own mind's voice and words! Now I don't want to confuse you by the statement "so-called process of thinking," because we actually do experience the real process of thinking from time to time. It's just that it is extremely difficult to distinguish between the times we experience the real process of thinking, as opposed to the times we are experiencing the so-called process of thinking.

The reason why is because both are nothing more than the process of simple listening, followed almost simultaneously by visualization. Has anyone ever asked you to be quiet so that they can hear their self-think? Have you ever listened to someone convey a message to you, and then you responded to them by saying "I see what you are saying"?

To hear what you are saying is to listen to what you are thinking, and to see what a person is saying is to visualize what they are saying!

What I am about to say applies to both the clean and unclean spirit at work in us. When we are in the process of deciding to commit sins that we are not really feeling all that compelled to do, it's just that we do it so much, that it seems like the thing to do. When this happens, chances are the reason you are not feeling compelled is because you are NOT being compelled. This means you are experiencing the real process of thinking. I said I was only going to talk about the unclean spirit's methods of operation within us, but I can't help but say that the clean spirit's method of operation is identical. The only difference is the clean spirit compels you to do the right thing. Philippians 2:13 states, "For it is God which worketh in you both to will and to do of his good pleasure." What this means is the spirit of the Lord inside you causing you to want to do good, as well as also causing you to actually do good.

Now to arrive at the conclusion that you want to do, say or have anything, is evidence in itself of having been compelled either by self or some other means. So what this verse is saying is that it is God/clean spirit inside you compelling you to do good. And just like his counterpart, from time to time, he will intentionally refuse to compel you to do that which is good, and you, being in that situation, not feeling compelled by what we call our conscience, but you go ahead and decide to do the good thing, because you've done it so much it feels like the thing to do. This is a situation in which you are experiencing the real process of thinking!

There is a reason for both the clean and unclean spirit refusing to compel or persuade us from time to time. Remember we start out innocent spirits, living in a body with two other spirits, one clean and one unclean. Their objective is to convert us into either a clean or an unclean spirit like themselves. Now the only way for either of them to assess your progress, they have to take their hands off of you so-to-speak, in order to see if you not can you, but will you walk on your own. The unclean spirit does it to see if you will walk in the darkness on your own without him having to use his powers of persuasion to compel you to do it! The clean spirit does it to see if you will walk in the light on your own without him having to use what is called your conscience, to compel you to do it.

As this process goes on throughout our lives, two things happen; 1. We slowly develop in two separate ways, not necessarily at the same time, but in the same lifetime. 2. We do not choose which one we like to walk in, because we like to walk in them both. We choose which one we like to walk in THE MOST, sometimes knowingly and sometimes unknowingly. Let's go back to the subject of the unclean spirit only. The unclean spirit lives out his life inside our body. Anything we feel, *it feels, anything that we eat, it eats, anything that we drink, it drinks and anything that we see, it sees. I can't speak for a woman, but when a man passes by a woman, while in agreement with the clean spirit within him, he will attempt to coach himself through the procedure of Not starring! Not looking twice! BUT something inside us, not us, but something inside us demands that we take another look. Then before we can make it to the other side of the street, we are crushed under a difficult to explain kind of pressure, and we take that second look! We did not want to look, but the unclean spirits wanted to.*

I want to elaborate on incidents in the Bible where unclean spirits used different parts of the human body to perform different functions. What I am going to do is, I'm going to quote the following scriptures and dissect them as I go, in to point out every body-part the unclean spirits uses, as he uses it. Mark 3:11&12 states, 11 "And unclean spirits, when they saw him," (If the perfect question were to be asked, it would be, how were the unclean spirits able to see Jesus? And the answer would be, they used the eyes of the human's body they were living in.) "fell down before him," (How were the unclean spirits able to fall down before Jesus? They used the knees of the human's body they were living in.) "and cried, saying, Thou art the Son of God." (How were they able to talk? They used the tongue, and vocal cord of the human's body they lived in.) 12 "And he straitly charged them that they should not make him known." (If Jesus talked to them, how were they able to hear him? They used the ears of the human's body they lived in.)

Acts 19:13-16 states, 13 "Then certain of the vagabond Jews, exorcists, took upon them to call over them which had evil spirits the name of the Lord Jesus, saying we adjure you by Jesus whom Paul preacheth. 14 And there were seven sons of one Sceva, a Jew, and chief of the priest, which did so. 15 And the evil spirit answered, and said, Jesus I know, and Paul I know; but who are ye?" How did the unclean spirit ask a question? He used the vocal cords of the human body he dwelled in, just as the apostle stated in Romans 7:20 "… …., it is no more I that do it, but sin that dwells in me."

Before I go further, I should explain something; there are two very different understandings of the word sin; 1. To disobey the law of God, knowingly or unknowingly. 2. Another name for one or more unclean spirits! So when Paul says "the sin that dwelleth in me," he is really saying (the unclean spirit that dwelleth in me) 16 "And the man in whom the evil spirit was leaped on them, and overcame them, and prevailed against them; so that they fled out of that house naked and wounded." How was the unclean/evil spirit able to attack, wound *and defeat seven men? Answer. He used the feet, fist, teeth, elbow, head, knees, fingernails, and whatever else body parts of the human's body it dwelled in, that it saw fit to perform the task.*

I pointed out all of these incidents in which unclean spirits used different parts of the human anatomy in a very evident way. The reason was to pave the way for what I am about to say! And that is, they also use the human anatomy in ways that are not evident at all. A spirit is invisible, and a glass of water is very visible. If I attempt to give an unclean spirit a glass of water, I am going to fail, no matter how many times I try. Now the unclean spirit is real, and the glass of water is real and, ironically enough, what makes this procedure impossible is reality itself. The reality is that they are in two different worlds. The only way for these two to be together is for one of them to enter into the world in which the other is already in. When that happens, the unclean spirit can drink the water and become instantly gratified. Jesus said in (Matthew 12:43) "When the unclean spirit is gone out a man, he walketh through dry places, seeking rest, and findeth none." The water the unclean spirit is seeking is indeed gratification in one of its many forms.

There is an old saying that goes, "Variety is the spice of life." But an even truer saying would be, "The variety of life's many gratifications is the true spice of life." The key word is gratification, and if we think that to quench its thirst for water is the only form of gratification an unclean spirit can and does experience inside the human body, then we are wrong, DEADLY wrong. I am a spirit, and because I have not yet lost my body, if I thirst for water I can quench my spirit's thirst by using my veil, which is to say, by using my fleshly body. The Bible speaks in Luke 16:24 about a man's spirit that wanted water, but because he had lost his Body, he could not quench his soul's thirst. (Luke 16:24) "And he cried and said, Father Abraham, have mercy on me, and send Lazarus, that he may dip the tip of his finger in water, and cool my tongue; for I am tormented in this flame."

By way of a live human body the two worlds are connected together, the spirit world and the physical world. Any form of gratification that an unclean spirit desires to experience, can be accomplished if the unclean spirit can enter a person. Any pleasure you feel, it or they feel also. That is why if you even so much as think about sex, your body feels a gratifying sensation instantly. It is also why you experience much difficulty blocking those thoughts at inconvenient times; even while praying at home or church. They also cause you to perceive reading the Bible as boring, causing you to doze off to sleep while reading it. When in fact, it is not you who is bored with reading the word of God, it's the unclean spirit that dwells inside you that is bored with the word of God!

Before I say anything else, I want to say this; The unclean spirits that I am going to be talking about in these next few paragraphs are not the one that we are born with. These are the ones we accumulate while walking in darkness, spiritual darkness. In other words, when we are sinning or when we are meditating on a sin or relishing the thought of sinning.

A good example would be, day dreaming about fornication or adultery. Also stealing or using your mind to prepare a lie, just in case you need to lie; so you won't have to try to think of a lie on the spot. To do these things, you have to stop walking in the spiritual light, and enter into spiritual darkness. Instantly! The sad truth is that it is not hard for an unclean spirit to enter a person. We humans take on unclean spirits like a dog takes on fleas. The dog wanders into places where there are fleas and as a result it gets fleas all over it. It does not get to choose which fleas it wants on it or how many.

We humans are the same way except we seem to think we can control what demons we take on by controlling what sins we participate in. But what many of us don't know is that no sin has ever taken place in the

Light. All sin takes place in the darkness. Demons or unclean spirits, whichever you prefer to call them, live in darkness at all times. When we walk off into the darkness, we enter into their world, where their rules apply. Their number one rule is try to cause us to lose our lives, and if Grace prevents them from taking our life, then it starts working on establishing a stronghold on the inside us.

When it comes down to a list of all the reasons why unclean spirits desire to enter us, I will start with one I am sure I have mentioned before.

1. When an unclean spirit enters into a person, it enters into another time zone. At this day in time it leaves a world where it has a day or two left to live freely before being thrown into the lake of fire, and enters into a world where it has one or two thousand years left to live freely before being cast into the lake of fire. If you can't see the advantage in that, then look at it this way. If a judge sentenced you to the electric chair and asked you do you want to be electrocuted in two days or in two thousand years from now, which would you chose?

2. When the devil and all his angles were kicked out of heaven, they did not have a house to live in; which is to say, they did not have a body to live inside. The human body was and still is the only body on earth specifically designed for God himself or the offspring of

God to dwell in. This also includes the Holy Spirit. Imagine for a moment that you died in the woods somewhere, and you didn't go to heaven. The body you used to live in is lying on the ground, ice cold, stiff as a board, with eyes wide open. So you are left with a choice, go burn in hell, go live in an animal such as a pig, a dog, a cow, or something like that. Or would you rather wait until a human being comes along and find a way to enter into him or her! Now do you understand one of the main reasons why they chose us?

3. The only way for an unclean spirit to enjoy its life is to enter a person's body. What I mean by enjoy its life is sex, alcohol, drugs, living like he has only one life left to live, so he lives it up, because it is true. The unclean spirit that lives inside us does have only one life left to live. He has already used up the other life he had in heaven, and so the earth is his final shot.

We, on the other hand, do have another life to live. So we have to start living like we do have another life to live! And if we find, after a close self-examination, that we are in fact, living as though we only have this one life to live, and then know this. The unclean spirit that is in you is using you to enjoy what is left of the only life he has left. You and I have another life to live, but only if we live like we have another life to live!

4. The other incentive that an unclean spirit has is the fact that if he succeeds in causing a person to be unsuitable for the kingdom of Heaven, it will buy him more time. Let me explain, there is a number that God the Father, and no one else knows. That number is the number of saints who will enter heaven. When that number is met, no one else will be allowed to enter into everlasting life in the kingdom. So the more people fail to enter Heaven, the more the evil spirits can prolong their time before being cast into the fire! Because the world won't end until the Lord lets in the number of souls he plans to let in. Mark 13:32 states, "But of that day and that hour knoweth no man, no, not the angels which are in heaven, neither the son, but the father." This scripture is referring to that number.

More than 99% of the world's population has had an outright disagreement with an unclean spirit without recognizing it! Here is a scenario in which it is more likely that we would be able to recognize both the second and the third party. Let us just say that someone does something to you or against you, and you are very angry. You get quiet while you are concentrating on how you will get even with them or go to where they live and do something to them. You get in your vehicle, alone with no one else in the vehicle, and you start out on your way to go and do something to the person. Remember, there is no one in the car but you. Then the *voice of reason begins to reason with you about the trouble you will most likely get into, or that it would be a sin to go through with this plan. So the voice of reasoning seems to be the way to go, so you say, verbally, "Nah, I'm not gonna do this." You turn the truck or car around and go back home.*

Now since you were driving alone in the car or truck when you made the statement, "Nah I'm not gonna do this." the question I would ask you is, who where you talking to? Before you answer, you should know this. The enemy would have you to believe you were talking to yourself, rather than for you to come into the knowledge that you were actually engaged in conversation with the enemy. This knowledge would also reveal the unclean spirit's location, which is inside you. You see it is easier to recognize his voice when you disagree with him, than when you agree with him. Because when we agree with whatever the unclean spirit says to do, it seems even more like it was or is your very own idea!

There are also times when we verbally disagree with the voice of reason/clean spirit, and there is no one around. We are alone and the clean spirit is trying to convince us to forgive someone, and we say out loud, something like, "I know it's wrong, but I just can't let him, or her get away with that." Once again the question is, who were you talking to, since there was no one in the car or truck but you? I do not want any of the readers to say that I said that it is not possible for a person to talk to his or her self, because we can and we do. For example, we sometimes use a combination of our mind and physical vocal cords, as well as the combination of our mind and spiritual vocal cord, by repeating a statement or group of numbers over and over to try to ensure we do not forget them.

There are a number of drugs in the world today that open windows in our temple/body, allowing unclean spirits to enter. Their demonic presence inside a person can range from mild to severe, depending on the drug, the amount, and it can also depend on the person. Alcohol, when consumed in moderation, can produce a controlled desired effect. But to become drunk is to become out of control, meaning we are temporarily not the one in control of the temple we live in. And if we are not in control, then who is? Answer. Unclean spirits. A person can be 20% in control of their self, and the demonic spirits 80% in control, which means the person is almost entirely under demonic control.

There is a difference between demonic control and demonic influence. Demonic influence is when the unclean spirit, or spirits, that live inside us daily, are not strong enough to control us. They influence us to drink enough alcohol or use the right drug to open up a window, which allows more than enough unclean spirits in to take control. Then that is exactly what they do, they take control and try to kill you, which by the way, they have experienced quite a bit of success with this particular method. Demonic influence almost always leads to demonic possession.

The demonic possession I am talking about in this case is alcohol and drug-related. It is at its strongest point during the period in which the person is under the influence of the drug or excess of alcohol. Once the person comes down off of the alcohol or drug, the window closes and the demonic unclean spirits are almost all forced out. I say almost all because some of them remain and join forces with the ones already living there, causing the demonic influence to become even stronger. When a person begins to feel him or herself coming down from the drug, crack cocaine, they become immediately gripped by an over powering sense of tremendous dread. Because of this dread, they will do almost anything to get more of the drug. But their uncontrollable desire to have more is not based upon any form of sound reasoning. Because the only thing that will happen to the person if he or she cannot get more of the drug, is they will return to being sober and in their right mind. Being sober, and in your right mind, is not something a human being should be desperately dreading!

So the question is, what and where is the source of the tremendous dread the person is experiencing? The answer is demons, devils or some people like to use the term, unclean spirits. When an unclean spirit is about to be kicked out of a person, he goes into a state of panic and tremendous dreading. A good illustration of this would be Mark chapter 5, verses 7 and 12, through 15. In (Mark 5:7&12-15) it states, 7."And cried with a loud voice, and said, What have I to do with thee, Jesus, thou Son of the most high God? I adjure thee by God, that thou torment me not." 12. "And all the devils besought him, saying, Send us into the swine, that we may enter them. 13. And forth with Jesus gave them leave. And the unclean spirits went out, and entered into the swine: and the herd ran violently down a steep place into the sea, (they were about two thousand;) and were choked in the sea. 14. And they that fed the swine fled, and told it in the city and in the country. And they went out to see what it was that was done. 15. And they come to Jesus, and see him that was possessed with the devil, and had the legion, sitting, and clothed, and in his right mind: and they were afraid."

Remember, demonic influence and demonic possession are two different things. In Matthew 12:45 Jesus speaks on the subject of demonic influence growing stronger. Matthew: 12:45 states, "Then goeth he, and taketh with himself seven other spirits more wicked than himself, and they enter in and dwell there: and the last state of that man is worse than the first. Even so shall it be also unto this wicked generation."

If you pay close attention to this verse, you will notice it is the demon that already lives there, who devises a method of getting seven more demons, more wicked than himself, to move in with him. What is that method? Demonic Influence! Sexual demonic influence is our adversary's number one weapon. The reason why is because it can start out as sexual demonic influence, and in five minutes or less, it can blossom into full grown sexual demonic possession. This can end in masturbation, incest, rape, adultery and the combination of rape and murder. King David fell victim to the same thing, sexual demonic influence, which very quickly turned into sexual demonic possession, resulting in adultery and murder of an innocent man! In (2nd Samuel: 11:2-5) it states, 2 "And it came to pass in an evening tide, that David arose from off his bed, and walked upon the roof of the king's house: and from the roof he saw a woman washing herself; and the woman was very beautiful to look upon. 3 And David sent and enquired after the woman. And one said, Is not this Bath-she-ba, the daughter of E-li-am, the wife of U-ri-ah the Hit-tite? 4 And David sent messengers, and took her; for she was purified from her uncleanness: and she returned unto her house. 5 And the woman conceived, and sent and told David, and said, I am with child."

When a person does these things, he or she is out of control, and if he or she is out of control, guess who is in control! The dictionary definition of the word possession is (control over oneself, one's mind, etc.)The dictionary definition of the word influence is (to move or impel (a person) to some action; persuade.)

Most stores that sell liquor, have advertisement signs that read (we sell spirits); which means they sell liquor. But the liquor, in and of itself, contains no spirits. But it opens windows that would be otherwise kept closed, and the spirits then rush in by themselves.

An example of a drug that results in instant demonic possession or control when used is crack cocaine. All of its users say it is the devil! Well I can understand why and how they came to that conclusion, but the devil is invisible to a human being, but crack cocaine is not. Sex is the number one weapon that the devils use against mankind and it is the only reason why crack cocaine is forced to be ranked the number two weapon used by demons against mankind! What makes a weapon most affective in the devil's hand is its level of addictiveness. Who do you know that experienced sex successfully for the first time, and did not become instantly addicted?

Many will say that, yes, their first sex experience was successful, but they gradually became addicted. The real truth is they became addicted instantly and gradually came to realize it and simply can't tell the difference between instantly and gradually! Crack cocaine is the exact same way!

Chapter 8

The One Thing Jesus Knew That We Do Not

The reason why I titled this chapter what Jesus knew that we do not is because when the time came for Jesus to be sacrificed on the cross, he had firsthand knowledge of the place he was about to go to. What I mean when I say he had firsthand knowledge is this. In the first part of (Genesis 1:26), it states, "And God said, Let us make man in our image,… … … … .." This means at least two beings, the Father and Son, made man.

The Lord also has revealed to me that, indeed, there was a third being there from the beginning, and that third being was the Holy Spirit. Proverbs 8:22&23 states, 22 "The Lord possessed me in the beginning of his way, before his works of old. 23 I was set up from everlasting, from the beginning, or ever the earth was." If you read all of Proverbs Chapter#8 you will find that the being doing the speaking refers to itself as Wisdom, yet it does not claim to have thought the Lord God, nor does it claim to have been thought by the Lord God. Yet it does claim to have been there even before the beginning.

Now Jesus, on the other hand, although he was there from the beginning, he did however state that he learned everything he knows from God the Father! So Jesus is not Wisdom, nor is God the Father, yet neither of them is without Wisdom. John 1:1&3) states, 1 "In the beginning was the Word, and the Word was with God, and the Word was God. 3 All things were made by him; And without him was not anything made that was made." This means that Jesus the Son and God the Father worked together along with Wisdom, (which is the Holy spirit), making everything that was and is made. In John chapter 1 verse number three, it starts off with the word all, which means that Jesus himself had a hand in the creation of Hell itself. Since Jesus himself helped build Hell itself, that means he knew exactly how the unimaginable pains of Hell would feel. For the sake of the title of this chapter, I am going to go ahead and acknowledge the fact that this is the one thing Jesus knew that we do not know, which is he knew exactly how it would feel to be in the fires of hell.

I would like to add another piece of information to help clarify your understanding of the role imagination plays in our fears. 1. If a person fears that five bad things will happen to them, and the five bad things do indeed happen, then that means they have what I call an accurate imagination. 2. If a person fears three bad things will happen to them, when in fact six bad things will happen to them, then that would be what I call an underactive imagination.

3. If a person fears 10 bad things will happen to them, when in fact only seven bad things happen, then that would be what I call an overactive imagination. Due to the fact that no human being has the capacity to accurately imagine what it is like to be in the fires of hell, then whatever he or she imagines is the result of an underactive imagination!

So whatever we imagine it to be like, the truth is we are not even close! No pleasure on the earth can be compared to the pleasure in heaven, and no pain on the earth can be compared to the pain in hell, nor the lake of fire. But before I go any further I want to say this about Jesus; Jesus was, and still is the boldest and the bravest man on earth and in heaven. Fear is something he NEVER experienced. Revelation 5:2-5 states, 2 "And I saw a strong angel proclaiming with a loud voice, who is worthy to open the book, and to loose the seals thereof? 3 And no man in heaven, nor in earth, neither under the earth, was able to open the book, neither to look thereon. 4 And I wept much, because no man was found worthy to open and to read the book, neither to look thereon. 5 And one of the elders saith unto me, Weep not: behold, the lion of the tribe of Juda, the Root of David, hath prevailed to open the book, and to lose the seven seals thereof." This proves that he was the boldest on earth and in heaven.

Now I said that because I need to draw attention to the fact that he was and still is the bravest man ever. Now that we are focusing on his bravery, let us now examine his conduct or behavior. In (Mark 14:33-36) it states, 33 "And he taketh with him Peter and James and John and began to be sore amazed, and to be very heavy;" (this verse is saying that he was extremely distressed and saddened.) 34 "And saith unto them, My soul is exceeding sorrowful unto death: tarry ye here, and watch." (In this verse Jesus is saying he is extremely bothered by what is about to take place) 35 "And he went forward a little, and fell on the ground, and prayed that, if it were possible, the hour might pass from him. 36 And he said, Abba, Father, all things are possible unto thee; take away this cup from me : nevertheless not what I will, but what thou wilt."

In these two verses Jesus is saying, if there is any other way for us to do this, I would rather do it that way, instead of doing it this way, but let your will be done and not my will, and he said that because he was worried about the unimaginable pain he was about to suffer! The reason I used the term unimaginable pain is because it is possible for a man to imagine being beaten and whipped with a whip. It is also possible for a man to imagine being nailed to a cross. But it is not possible for a man to accurately imagine what the pain of the fires of hell feels like. Yet, on the contrary, with Jesus Christ it was possible for him to imagine exactly what it felt like because he was both man and God and not only that, remember, he helped build hell and its fires.

Another reason why I am led to use the term "unimaginable" is because the mind of man is limited in its ability to accurately imagine any number of things. For example, a man, woman or child may be able to imagine what it is like to live in the kingdom of heaven, but they cannot accurately imagine what it is like to live in the kingdom of heaven. In (1st Corinthians 2:9) it states, "But as it is written, Eye hath not seen, nor ear heard, neither have entered into the heart of man," (that means man cannot imagine it) "the things which God hath prepared for them that love him."

Herein lies the problem. We, as men, do not possess the ability to accurately imagine what it feels like to be in hell, nor the lake of fire. Yes, we do go ahead and imagine what it is like to be in hell, or the lake of fire, and because of our imagination of what it is like, we all *experience a level of fear. But due to the fact our imagination is inadequate on this particular subject, unfortunately that means that our level of fear is also inadequate!*

Proverbs 9:10 states, "The fear of the Lord is the beginning of wisdom: and the knowledge of the holy is understanding." If the fear of the Lord, which we have, is inadequate, then that means our understanding of the Lord is also inadequate! So the question is this; what must I do in order to obtain both a proper fear and a proper understanding of the Lord? The answer is this; Due to the fact that mankind, (with the exception of Jesus Christ) is unable to adequately imagine what it is like to be in either hell or the lake of fire, then we must focus on the conduct or behavior of the only man in the history of the world who was able to adequately imagine what it was like to be in the fires of hell. That man was Jesus Christ. Before going further, I want to take the time to say this; I do not want to give the impression that Jesus was not at all concerned about the physical pain and abuse his physical body would have to endure before he actually died. But what I am saying is that his major concern was the pain that he would have to endure after he died and received his celestial body, because the fires of hell were designed to inflict tremendous pain on the celestial body. In (Matthew10:28) Jesus himself said, "And fear not them which kill the body, but are not able to kill the soul: but rather fear him which is able to destroy both soul and body in hell." Now this statement applies to Christians also, only for us it would be the lake of fire instead of in hell.

I am not using Matthew 10:28 to try to indicate in any way that Jesus feared God the Father, nor am I trying to indicate that he feared the fire itself. There is a difference between fear and dread. In (Deuteronomy 1:29) Moses was talking to the children of Israel, and in his statement he is indicating that there is a difference between fear and dread. Deuteronomy 1:29 states, "Then I said unto you, Dread not, neither be afraid of them." He was advising them to not be overcome by these two different emotions; one being fear and the other being dread. In (1st John 4:18) it states, "There is no fear in love; but perfect love casteth out fear; because fear hath torment. He that feareth is not made perfect in love." And Jesus had perfect love toward the Father, so he had no reason at all to fear.

I used (Matthew 10:28) only to show what Jesus's priorities where at that time. Jesus did not experience fear at that time, but he was experiencing tremendous dread, because of his vivid imagination and foreknowledge of what the fires of hell would feel like. In (Luke 22:44) it states, "And being in agony he prayed *more earnestly: and his sweat was as it were great drops of blood falling down to the ground."*

The dictionary meaning of the word agony is extreme physical or mental suffering. The point that I am trying to make is this, if God the Son was 'SO' worried about the pain and torment that he was about to have to endure in the fires of hell, that he talked to the Father about doing it another way, and even after the Father sent an angel from heaven to strengthen him, he was still in extremely serious agony over what was about to happen to him! Now I don't know about anyone else, but what that tells me is this; if Jesus was worried to that extreme about dying and going into the fires of hell, then I myself should be a whole heck of a lot more worried now, than I was, before the Holy Spirit pointed this out to me!

As we focus on Jesus's behavior in the situation he was in, do not forget to focus on this one additional factor. Jesus knew beforehand that he would only have to suffer in the fires of hell for just a little while. Exactly how long that little while lasted we do not know. But I do know that it was a matter of hours or minutes, and not days. The reason why I said it was a matter of hours or minutes is because in (Luke 23:43) it states, "And Jesus said unto him, Verily I say unto thee, Today shalt thou be with me in paradise."

Another piece of proof that paradise is located in the center of the earth where hell is located is the fact that, by his own admission, while hanging on the cross, he stated that he would be in paradise that same day. So by this we know for sure that he was indeed in paradise, but when he rose from the grave on the third day, he told Mary Magdalene not to touch him because he had not yet ascended to his Father. (The word ascended means gone up.) So if he had previously been located in paradise and had not yet gone up to see the Father who is located in heaven, then that proves this paradise was not located in heaven. Now for Jesus to be in paradise that same day, it would mean that he stayed in the lowest hell for time duration of only hours or minutes.

Let me start by saying this, in hell there are two compartments, which are divided by a great gulf to keep them separated one from another. In one compartment there is pain and suffering. The Bible describes this place as the lowest hell. (Proof) In (Psalms 86:13) it states, "For great is thy mercy toward me: and thou hast delivered my soul from the lowest hell".

The other side is called paradise. (Proof) In (Luke 16:22-26) it states, 22 "And it came to pass, that the beggar died, and was carried by the angels into Abraham's bosom: the rich man also died, and was buried; 23

And in hell he lift up his eyes, being in torments, and seeth Abraham afar off, and Lazarus in his bosom." If you will notice, in verse 23 it states that the rich man was in hell, yet he was having a conversation with father Abraham, which means that they were both in hell. Also, the rich man looked upward in order to see father Abraham. So if the rich man had to look up to see Abraham, that would mean the rich man was in a location lower than the location Abraham and Lazarus were located, which proves that the rich man was located in the lowest hell. 24 *"And he cried and said, Father Abraham, have mercy on me, and send Lazarus, that he may dip the tip of his finger in water, and cool my tongue; for I am tormented in this flame. 25. But Abraham said, Son, remember that thou in thy lifetime receivedst thy good things, and likewise Lazarus evil things: but now he is comforted, and thou art tormented. 26 And beside all this, between us and you there is a great gulf fixed: so that they which would pass from hence to you cannot; neither an they pass to us, that would come from thence."*

Isaiah 53:7 states, "He was oppressed, and he was afflicted, yet he opened not his mouth: he was brought as a lamb to the slaughter, and as a sheep before her shearers is dumb, so he openeth not his mouth." This does not mean that he never spoke one word throughout the entire ordeal he was going through. What this means is that he never opened his mouth to defend himself or to protest against what was being done to him. Let us not forget what it is that we are doing here, we are keeping the focus on his behavior! So with that being said; starting from the moment they apprehended him, beat him with their hands, put a crown of thorns on his head, beat him with a whip and nailed him to the cross, he never said a word to defend himself. So he did exactly what the scriptures prophesied he would do.

However, when his soul begin to enter into the fires of hell, he cried out with a loud voice, because of the pain. Mark 15:37&39 states, 37 "And Jesus cried with a loud voice, and gave up the ghost." 39 "And when the centurion, which stood over against him, saw that he so cried out, and gave up the ghost, he said, Truly this man was the Son of God."

For many years the significance of Jesus crying out the way he did, and at the time that he did it, has been somewhat of a mystery, mainly because for number one, he did not cry out while the soldiers beat him with their hands. Number two, he did not cry out when they beat him with a whip. And number three, he did not cry out when they drove nails into his hands and feet. So to the natural man it doesn't make sense for him to wait until all the pain and suffering is over, and then cry out.

If it had been me, I half way believe that I could somehow manage to not cry out while they beat me with their hands, but I know that I would have cried out when they whipped me with the whip. I most likely would have passed out when they began to drive nails into my hands and feet.

So the question is this; if he was strong enough to endure being tortured like that without ever crying out, then why would he wait until all the pain and suffering were over and then cry out? Answer. At the point where we thought his pain and suffering was over, that was actually the point where his true pain and suffering began. Because it was at that point that his soul was in the process of entering into the actual fires of hell; literally! What I mean by "in the process of entering into Hell" is this; Jesus was entering into death as we know it, so part of him was in hellfire and part of him was still on the earth. In other words, his soul was in departing.

A classic example of what I am trying to say would be in Genesis 35:17&18 where it states, 17 "And it came to pass, when she was in hard labour, that the midwife said unto her, Fear not; thou shalt have this son also. 18 And it came to pass, as her soul was in departing, (for she died) that she called his name Ben-o'-ni: but his father called him Benjamin." The point I am trying to bring out is this, Rachel's soul had not yet completely left her body when she named her last child, and likewise, Jesus's soul had not yet completely left his body when he yelled out, because of the pain he was in, having partially entered into the flames of hell fire!

One of the reasons why Jesus had to go to the location in hell where there is pain and suffering, which is called the lowest hell, was this: The only way to take the place of a person who dies in their sin is to first die the physical death in their stead and then burn in hell fire in their stead also. Ephesians 4:9 states, "(Now that he ascended, what is it but that he also descended first into the lower parts of the earth?" This is Paul's way of saying that Jesus descended into the lowest hell first, and then on the third day he ascended up to the Father, (after talking to Mary Magdalene.)

Now I have said all that to say this; Out of all the foreknowledge that Jesus had, none of it affected him the way the foreknowledge of what it would be like to enter into the fires of hell, even though it was for only a time span of either minutes or hours! Don't forget, Jesus also had the foreknowledge of the fact that he would be in paradise on the same day, shortly after he entered the flames.

When we re-examine Jesus's conduct in Luke 22:41-44, we find evidence of a tremendous state of dreading on Jesus's part. The situation was one of two things, either it was as bad as he acted like it was going to be, or he was only acting like it was going to be that bad. If he was only acting, then that would mean he was guilty of DECEPTION , which means that he was deceiving you and me by way of his conduct. Now that would be a SIN, and we know he never sinned. So that leads us to only one conclusion, and that is, "It really was as dreadful a situation as his conduct indicated."

The average person would think it should have been of some consolation to him, the fact that he already knew he wouldn't have to stay in the fire very long. But his conduct indicated that it was not much of a consolation to him at all! Luke 22:41-44 states, 41 "And he was withdrawn from them about a stone's cast, and he kneeled down, and prayed, 42 Saying, Father, if thou be willing, remove this cup from me: nevertheless not my will, but thine, be done. 43 And there appeared an angel unto him from heaven, strengthening him. 44 And being in an agony he prayed more earnestly: and his sweat was as it were great drops of blood falling down to the ground."

I don't know what that angel told Jesus, but I do know that I myself was in a vision, and in this vision an angel came to me, and he was very tall. I would say about 9½ feet tall at least. There are more details to this vision but I will not go into them right now. What I want to share with you is the seriousness of the expression on his face when he looked me directly in the eyes and told me, "you have to be strong". That happened a few years ago, and the full impact of his facial expression did not hit me then. But every time I would think about the look on his face, it became more and more clear to me that his eyes were looking at something that I never ever- ever want to see, and most assuredly do not want to experience. He said, "Be strong!"

Now to those of us who understand the word, to us it truly is a fearful thing to fall into the hands of the living God. It is this fear that will not allow us to relax and enjoy ourselves when we know we are walking in DARKNESS! But to those of us who do not understand the word, we do not fear the darkness very much at all, even though we have accepted Jesus Christ as our Lord and savior, we still visit the darkness quite frequently while thinking in the back of our minds, "I know that what I am about to do is wrong. So when I get through, I will wait a couple of days to allow the good Lord time to get past his anger and disappointment with me and then I will apologize and ask for his forgiveness!"

P.S. sounds like a clever plan! But will I always have that badly needed couple of days to smooth things over with the Lord?

Chapter 9

In A Nut Shell #One

If I were to try to sum it all up I guess I would say the good Lord offered Adam a choice between Life and a sample of Life. He even went so far as to command Adam to choose Life. But in spite of the Lord's command Adam chose the sample of Life instead of actual Life itself.

I know that some will say that Adam did not act alone in this decision. However, the truth is whatever the Lord God All Mighty says the truth is! You see in King James Version (Genesis 5:2) it states, "Male and female created he them; and blessed them, and called their name Adam, in the day when they were created."

If you reexamine the verse you will see that God made male and female, that's two. It says, "created he them," the word (them) is plural, meaning more than one, "and blessed them." Once again the word (them) is plural, meaning more than one, "and called their." The word their is also plural, meaning more than one, "name." The word (name) is a single word, meaning only one name. Not (names), which would be plural. "Adam" Adam is the single name that God gave his single creation.

He did not name them man, as some translations have because man is not a name! Although God divided Adam into two parts or halves, it did not stop Adam from being Adam in God's eyes. It was both halves of Adam that chose the sample of Life instead of Life itself.

Now if any of us living this sample of Life would like to correct The Creator on his selection of words, then go right ahead!

Chapter 10

In A Nut Shell #Two

I had a mental vision of me and the Lord high upon a mountain, and the Lord showed me my whole life from the time I was born up unto that point. He asked me, "Do you like the small sample of life that you have lived so far?" I said yes. Then he asked me "Do you want life?" So I opened my mouth to say yes; but before I could move my lips or fix my tongue to utter a word, he took his hand and put it over my mouth. Then he placed a book in my hands. I asked him what the book was for. Then he said to me "This book will show you how to answer yes to the question that I asked you and this book will also show you how to answer no to the question I asked you.

If anyone else in heaven or on earth would have asked you this question, then you would have been able to answer the question with a simple verbal yes or verbal no, but because I myself have asked you the question, it can only be answered with a living yes or a living no. In other words, you have to live a yes or you have to live no! If you want life, all you have to do is answer yes *to the question. If you do not want life, all you have to do is answer no to the question. It is just that simple.*

He said, "From now until the hour I take you away from the earth, whether you are able to recognize it or not, you and I are going to be engaged in a conversation in which you will be explaining to me why you do not want Life, and how you think it should be. Or we will be engaged in a conversation in which you will be explaining to me why you do want life, and at the end of the conversation you have my word that you will get your wish.

Go and tell everyone in the world that I myself have asked them the same question! Mouth need not open and tongue need not utter!

(I had a mental vision.)

Chapter 11

In A Nut Shell #Three

There is a reason why more females are born into this world than males. Not in every family, but from the beginning of the world until now. In my family there were four boys, myself, Rodney, Tyrone, little Henry and one girl, Dorothy. There is a reason why females live longer than males. There is a reason why the angels from heaven came down to be with the daughters of men.

Genesis 6:2 states, "That the sons of God saw the daughters of men that they were fair; and they took them wives of all which they chose." The angels that did this got in big trouble for doing it. Jude 1:6 states, "And the angels which kept not their first estate, but left their own habitation, he hath reserved in everlasting chains under darkness unto the judgment of the great day".

When Adam first saw Eve he wasn't the only one relieved to see a female. You see there is nothing in heaven but males. It has always been that way, but the new heaven will be totally different in that respect. Females made it possible for man to have a little piece of heaven on earth. Females are already the anticipated addition to the kingdom that will revolutionize the definition of the word heaven.

Females live longer than men. Not because men take more risk, nor any kind of genetic shortcoming. Women love more. They give more. They sacrifice their beautiful bodies to give birth to a child, even if they have already decided not to keep the child. They forgive infidelity at a rate of 10 to 1 over men. It appears that when women love, it is almost blind. They seem for the most part to be unaffected by the un-loyal-ness, selfishness or down-right no-goodness of the person they love.

The reason they out live men is because they are more suitable for the kingdom. Proverbs 3:2&3 states, "For length of days, and long life, and peace, shall they add to thee. Let not mercy and truth forsake thee: bind them about thy neck; write them upon the table of thine heart:" Now I can understand why the sons of God could not wait.

When the war in heaven was over, one third of its population was gone. Revelation 12:4&7-8 states, 4 "And his tail drew the third part of the stars of heaven,…… .." 7 "And there was war in heaven: Michael and his angels fought against the dragon; and the dragon fought and his angels, 8 And prevailed not; neither was their place found any more in heaven."

This left heaven in need of repopulating. We are the ones that will repopulate heaven, but not with all males. Matthew 19:28 states, "And Jesus said unto them, Verily I say unto you, That ye which have followed me, in the regeneration when the son of man shall sit in the throne of his glory, ……… " So in the end there is someone for everyone!

Chapter 12

Burying your Talent

Many Christians go about their life from day to day feeling that their salvation is secure. But what they don't know is that we have work we must do as Christians. Through our verbal instruction and physical involvement in another person's life we have to win people to Christ or win them back to Christ. To talk to a person and get them to except Jesus Christ as their Lord and savior can sometimes involve a little bit of work.

Once we get a person to go ahead and get saved, some of us have a tendency to think our duty as a Christian is fulfilled. But the truth is we have only begun. Introducing a person to Christ is like giving someone a baby tree, when the person doesn't know anything at all about trees. You see, when the Lord comes for that person you introduced to Christ, #1.That person's tree must be alive. # 2. It must be bearing fruit. If we know how to keep our own tree alive and bearing fruit, then we must take the time to show them how to keep their tree alive and producing fruit.

The person you bring to Christ is your work in Christ. In fact it is indeed what you do for a living, eternal-living! If you are a doctor or a lawyer, then that means you bring people to Christ for a living and you practice law or medicine on the side! You are someone else's work in Christ. Here in America it is rare to find a person who does not know the Lord, because we are a Christian nation. But we do run across a person every now and then that hasn't accepted Christ. Most of the work in Christ that we will be receiving credit for will be people who are already Christians, but they have back slid in one way or another. No one person can receive all the credit for saving someone else's soul, but you can receive credit ranging from a small amount of credit for saving someone's soul to most of the credit for saving someone's soul.

The reason why no one person can claim all the credit for saving some one's soul is because we work side by side with the Father, the Son and the Holy Spirit. So we have to share the credit for whatever work we do with who ever works right along beside us. The Holy Spirit has caused me to understand that people do not learn by listening. They learn by seeing. Listening does play a role, but seeing is by far the best and most effective tool in the work that we do. So for the best results we have to show a brother or a sister or a child how to get to heaven, instead of telling them how to get there.

In (1st Corinthians 3:13-15) it states, 13 "Every man's work shall be made manifest: for the day shall declare it, because it shall be revealed by fire; and the fire shall try every man's work of what sort it is. 14 If any man's work abides which he hath built thereupon, he shall receive a reward. 15 If any man's work shall be burned, he shall suffer loss: but he shall be saved; yet so as by fire." In verse 13 Paul is saying that everyone's work of leading people to Christ, as well as their work in being instrumental in causing people to remain in Christ, is going to be put to the test. In verse 14 Paul is saying that, of the people you worked on in your life time, all those who make it into the kingdom that you worked on; you will be rewarded for them if you yourself make it into the kingdom. In verse 15 Paul is saying, if any of the people that you worked on do not make it into the kingdom, then you will not get a reward for them. He is also saying, if some of the people you worked on fail to enter the kingdom; this does not mean that you yourself will be disqualified from being excepted into the kingdom.

You have to remember that you yourself are also somebody else's work in Christ. After all you did not introduce yourself to Christ! In fact, you are a number of other people's work in Christ. Because more than one person will have contributed to your making it into the kingdom ----IF YOU MAKE IT IN!

In 1st Corinthians 9:1 Paul ask four rhetorical questions, which is to say, they weren't really questions, but rather statements. With that having been said, it is the fourth statement that I draw your attention to. In his fourth statement he said, "are not ye my work in the Lord?" In other words Paul is telling them that they are his work. In 1st Corinthians 3:13-15, Paul is explaining to them all about work. In First Corinthians 9:1 he tells them that they are his work.

When the scripture says that your work will be tried by fire, it means that it will be tried by God. Hebrews 12:29 states, "For our God is a consuming fire." Deuteronomy 4:24 states, "For the Lord thy God is a consuming fire, even a jealous God."

If your works make it into the kingdom, but for some reason you yourself do not make it; then your reward will be given to someone who did make into the kingdom. Now if you don't believe that you can help other people enter the kingdom, and you yourself be denied, then read (1st Corinthians 9:27) where Paul says, "But I keep under my body, and bring it into subjection: lest that by any means, when I have preached to others, I *myself should be a castaway."* Paul is saying that no matter how many people he leads to Christ; if he does not conduct himself like Christians should conduct themselves, then he himself will not be accepted into the kingdom of heaven!

In (Matthew 25:14-30) Jesus is going to explain what is going to happen to people who receive the gift of salvation, but because they were either too lazy or too fearful, they did not try to pass the gift on to anyone but themselves. In other words, they took the talent the Lord gave them, which is the gift of salvation and buried it in the ground. He also makes mention of taking whatever reward the unapproved has and giving it to the approved.

Matthew 25:14-30 states, 14 *"For the kingdom of heaven is as a man travelling into a far country, who called his own servants, and delivered unto them his goods. 15 And unto one he gave five talents, to another two, and to another one; to every man according to his several ability; and straightway took his journey."*

It goes on to say, 16 *"Then he that received the five talents went and traded with the same, and made them other five talents. 17 And likewise he that had received two, he also gained other two. 18 But he that had re-*

ceived one went and digged in the earth, and hid his lord's money."

It continued to say, 19 "After a long time the lord of those servants cometh, and reckoneth with them. 20 And so he that had received five talents came and brought other five talents, saying, Lord, thou deliveredst unto me five talents, behold, I have gained beside them five talents more. 21 His lord said unto him, Well done thou good and faithful servant: thou has been faithful over a few things, I will make the ruler over many things: enter thou into the joy of thy lord. 22 He also that had received two talents came and said, Lord, thou deliveredst unto me two talents: behold I have gained two other talents beside them. 23 His lord said unto him, well done, good and faithful servant; thou has been faithful over a few things, I will make thee ruler over many things: enter thou into the joy of thy lord. 24 Then he which had received the one talent came and said, Lord, I knew thee that thou art an hard man, reaping ware thou hast not sown, and gathering where thou has not strawed: 25 And I was afraid, and went and hid thy talent in the earth: lo, there thou hast which is thine."

Then it went on to say, 26 "His lord answered and said unto him, thou wicked and slothful (lazy) servant, thou knewest that I reap where I sowed not, and gath-

ered where I have not strawed: 27 Thou oughtest therefore to have put my money to the exchangers, and then at my coming I should have received mine own with usury (interest). 28 Take therefore the talent from him, and give it unto him which hath ten talents. 29 For unto everyone that hath shall be given, and he shall have abundance: but from him that hath not shall be taken away EVEN THAT WHICH HE HATH. 30 And cast ye the unprofitable servant into outer darkness: there shall be weeping and gnashing of teeth."

You see, if you except the gift of salvation and never take the time to give that same gift to anyone but yourself, then that means you are the servant that buried his master's talent in the ground! I am going to be strait forward and to the point. Jesus is in the soul-saving business and if you work for Jesus, then you are in the soul-saving business also.

The five talents represent your pastor at your church. The one with the two talents represent the deacons in your church. The one with the one talent represents each individual in the congregation. The entire message is specifically to the congregation member.

The preacher knows his job is to bring people to Christ, sometimes 4, 5 or 6 at a time. The deacon knows his job is to bring people to Christ 1, 2 and sometimes 3 at a time. But the average regular congregation member does not seem to understand that his or her job is to bring people to Christ one at a time, at the very least!

When we come before the Judgment seat, the first question that will be asked of us is going to be, "Who did you bring with you?" Or, "How many did you bring with you?" If your answer to that question is, "Nobody, I just brought myself." then I know for a fact that I would not wish to be you at that particular moment in time!

Now to those of us who are shameful, bashful, shy and too lazy to get up, get out there and bring people to the Lord; this is what the Lord himself has to say about that. In (Revelation 21:8) it states, "But the fearful and unbelieving, and the abominable, and murders, and whoremongers, and sorcerers, and idolaters, and all liars, shall have their part in the lake which burneth with fire and brimstone: which is the second death."

Now to the person who happens to be shy or bashful, I say this; do not pick loud rambunctious type people to try to bring to Christ. Instead look for people like yourself, because you are the only one that people like yourself will trust. Then later on when you get used to it, then maybe you can try to reach out to the loud rambunctious type.

If after receiving this knowledge you feel a strange feeling that feels something like fear, then don't panic. Listen to this. Hebrews 10:31&35 states, 31 "It is a fearful thing to fall into the hands of the living God. 35 Cast not away therefore your confidence, which hath great recompense of reward. Paul said that we are co-workers along beside Christ, building the new kingdom. In (2nd Corinthians 6:1) it states "We then, as workers together with him... ... ..." We are not here as by-standers!

Chapter 13

Two Brothers & Profound Effect

This chapter starts with a parable about two brothers. A long-long time ago, there was this family, and they lived in a land where there was zero tolerance for a thief, regardless of age. The penalty for stealing anything was too gruesome to even mention, but for the sake of its importance to this chapter, I am going to give the details of the penalty. I use the word penalty instead of the word punishment. Because in the world we live in, punishment seems to imply correction, and where correction is applied, the guilty person is allowed to continue living. But the word penalty seems to always include the possibility, as well as the likelihood, of the death of the guilty person.

If it was determined a person had stolen something, the townspeople would form a mob. Then they would hunt for the thief until they found her or him. Wherever they found the person, grownup or child, they would first beat them with their hands and fists. Then they would have as many people as it took to hold the guilty person down, while another person beat them with a whip until they almost passed out. After this they would put a rope around their neck, throw the rope over a tree limb, and pull it until it is tight, but not tight enough to completely choke the guilty person or lift them off of the ground. Next, they would soak the person with lamp oil, from head to feet, then set them on fire, and watch them scream and jerk and wiggle. Then before the rope has a chance to burn too thin to support the guilty person's body weight, they go ahead and hang the person until they stop moving altogether. The body would be left hanging on the tree for their family to cut it down, if the guilty person had any family. The only break a woman would get was, if she was pregnant, they would lock her up until she had and weaned the child off breast milk.

As I was saying, a long-long time ago, there was a family, and they lived in a land where there was zero tolerance for a thief, regardless of age. One day the family had ran almost completely out of supplies. The situation was getting critical, and the father knew something had to be done. He had four children, and his wife was a little past nine months pregnant, and about to deliver any day now. He had two girls, one a year and a half old, and the other one two and a half years old. Of his two boys, one was 14 years old, and the other was six years old. After thinking the situation over, he decided the trip into town would take almost the better part of a whole day just getting there. Then he had to pick out all the supplies, load the wagon, tie it all down, then make the long journey back to their little farm. He had delivered all four of his own children himself, something he had learned from being raised by his grandmother, who was a midwife all of her life before she died.

The real problem was that they lived so far out that they had no neighbors for miles and miles around. So he had no choice but to seriously consider sending his oldest son, Travis, to town. Travis was only 14 years old, but it was clear to see that his oldest boy was going to make a fine young man someday! He was honest, hardworking and smart, too. As a matter of fact, Matthew, the boy's daddy, couldn't recall ever seeing or hearing tell of a boy catching on to how to do things, and maturing at as young a age as his son. Sometimes, when he would allow himself to think about how proud he was of that boy, it would bring tears to his eyes. He thought seriously about going ahead and teaching him how to deliver a baby when his youngest sister was born a year and a half ago, but he figured the boy was too young to be seeing his own mother naked. Now he really wished he would have went ahead and taught him, because he knew that he would have no problem trusting him to such a responsibility.

    That night he had a talk with his son, and explained the situation and made out a list, and told him to get to bed soon because he would have to pull out before sunrise. The boy had made the trip many times before with his dad, and knew what all he had to do. He had to make the trip starting before sunrise. Make it to town a little before sunset. Give the supply list and half the money to the store owner, so he can gather it all, and have it ready to load the wagon the next morning, at which time he would give the store owner the other half of the money. He would have to spend the night in the town horse stable, sleeping in the back of the wagon. There were some dangers to consider, but when you take into consideration the gruesome details of what happens to law breakers in this land, it was highly unlikely that anything would happen to the boy on the trail.

    So Travis went to bed early that night, and for some strange reason, so did little Adam; Travis's little brother. Even though Travis was 14, and Adam was only five; these two boys were pretty much inseparable ever since little Adam was about three years old. Everywhere Travis went on the little farm the boys were being raised on, there was little Adam tagging along behind him. Early the next morning Travis and his dad Matthew, eased out of the house and out to the barn to hitch up the mule. Well, before they even finished, there was little Adam with that lost puppy look in his eyes. Mat knew that this would surely happen if he and Travis weren't extra quiet getting out of the house that morning. Anyway it was too late; the cat was out of the bag now. So after much of what turned out to be failed efforts, against his better judgment, he decided to let the little boy go along with his big brother. Besides, it wouldn't be a half bad idea if Travis had some company on that long lonesome ride ahead of him.

Everything went as planned, they made it to town a little before sundown. The older boy gave the storeowner the list and half the money, and they spent the night in the stable, sleeping in the back of the wagon. When morning came, they went over to the store to pick up the supplies. While Travis and the storeowner, who seemed to be a mean character, were loading the wagon and securing the load, he had little Adam wait inside the store so that he wouldn't get in the way. Now the not-so-good part!

While little Adam was waiting inside the store, he saw a big jar at the end of the counter on the floor. He walked down to take a look at it, and lo-and-behold it was a candy jar. Little Adam grabbed the last two pieces of candy that were in the jar, and put them in his pocket. Well it just so happens that Matt, the boy's dad, would always get the boys some candy whenever he made the trip to town for supplies; so it was already on the list and already being loaded on the wagon with the rest of the supplies. The downside to that was the fact that it was fresh on the storeowner's memory, the fact that he had only two pieces of candy left in the jar. Because he almost forgot to include the candy, cause he kept it in the jar with the rest of the candy, so as to keep the ants from getting ahold of it, and he set the hold jar on the floor where he would see it in the morning and remember, instead of leaving it on the shelf where he normally keeps it.

So the boys took out for home with the wagon load of supplies. Meanwhile the store owner locked up the store, and went across the street for his usual coffee and breakfast, along with two or three hours of early morning gossip. Afterward he went back and opened the store, which is when he discovered the empty candy jar. He didn't know which of the two boys had taken the candy, but he would almost swear that it had to be the youngest one.

The boys got home a little after dark, washed up, had a late supper, talked a little, and finally fell asleep. The next day little Adam put his hand in his pocket and to his surprise, instead of finding two pieces of candy, he only found one. He looked and he looked, everywhere his little mind could think of. Finally he decided that he was just going to have to break his piece in half and he'd eat one half, and that way Travis could eat the other half. So he called Travis behind the barn to give him his piece. But when Travis saw the candy he asked little Adam where he had gotten the candy, and little Adam said their dad had given it to him. Well that didn't sound right because mom was the one who always rewarded the kids with sweets, and never ever before meal time, and it was almost supper time.

Meanwhile, the storeowner and a large group of men had just found the piece of candy that little Adam lost out of his pocket on the side of the only road that leads to the only house at the end of the road about a half hour from the house. To make matters even worse, the candy the storeowner had sold to them was red, but the two left in the jar were yellow.

At that very moment Travis felt a very sad-sick feeling deep in his chest. A feeling no 14-year-old boy should be feeling. But he wasn't sure yet as to whether his suspicions were correct. So he took little Adam by the hand, and ran into the house to ask his dad it he gave little Adam the candy. That is when little Adam started crying and confessed to what he had done. Travis had seen with his own two eyes, what happened to a 13-year-old girl for stealing, when he was only 10 years old himself. He saw it on one of his trips to town with his dad, and he never forgot it. Now little Adam knew it was wrong to steal, but he just didn't know how wrong.

While they were all standing in the kitchen, the storeowner and all the men with him came up in the front yard, and started walking toward the house. At that very moment it seemed as though a thousand things were running through Travis's mind. His mother was pregnant, his two little sisters couldn't take care of themselves, and his dad didn't even make the trip to town. Besides, the only one who could take care of the family was his dad. So he told Adam to hand him both pieces of the candy and he put them in his pocket and ran out the front door, shutting it behind him before anyone had a chance to say anything.

When he got outside he asked the men why they were here. Then the storeowner said we come to get that little brother of yours. For what, said Travis? For stealing candy out of my store. He didn't steal it, I did, said Travis. When he said that, they all grabbed him and started dragging him out into the middle of the front yard, at which point little Adam broke loose from his mother's arms, out the door, and threw a rock that hit the storeowner in the head, all the while screaming,

"Let my brother go"! About that time his father grabbed him and brought him back in the house, because everyone who ever tried to stop a lynching always got the same treatment.

They all jumped on the boy beating him with their fists. Then held him down while one of them started beating him with a horsewhip. After that they soaked his body in oil, set fire to it and hanged him by his neck, burning and choking until he died! Travis's mother went went into labor, and passed out. While his father was tending to her, little Adam stood in the doorway with tears in his eyes and saw it all. Little Adam lived to be 86 years old. The death of his big brother had such a profound effect on his life that from that day unto the day he died, not only did he never again steal anything, he also never again lied or so much as utter one curse word out of his mouth.

The three things that caused such a profound response on little Adam's life were #1. He talked with Travis, he walked with him and really got to know his big brother. #2. He loved him. And #3. He understood clearly, who Travis was and why he did what he did.

Now we come to the facts. The first part of Jeremiah 1:5 states, "Before I formed thee in the belly I knew thee; ……….". This statement in one way or another applies to every man or woman on the earth who proceeded fourth from God the father. This also includes the first and the second Adam. The wording would be a little different in the case of Adam, but the procedure was the exact same, as everyone else that left that world, which is heaven, and entered this world, which is earth. Chapter 3 of this book explains how the Lord creates a path for each of us and then takes us down every crack, nook and every turn of our individual path in order to see how every situation can possibly turn out, both positive and negative. Then we are formed in our mother's womb. Adam went through the same procedure before he was formed of the dust of the earth. Eve went through it before she was formed of Adam's rib. Jesus, who is the second Adam, also went through it. This is where prophecy comes from. This is how the good Lord can say I knew you before you were born. So the topic is going to be about the first and second Adam before they were formed!

The first thing we should know is that they both have the same daddy. Luke 3:38 states, "Which was the son of Enos, which was the son of Seth, which was the son of Adam, which was the son of God." Now according to my understanding, when two boys have the same daddy it means they are brothers. With that having been said let us move on to the before they were formed part. Before he laid the foundation of the earth, God the father *already had many sons. His first and oldest son was who we come to know as Jesus. He was the smartest, the boldest and the most loyal son that the good Lord had. There are no words in heaven nor earth that can begin to describe how proud he was (and still is) of that boy! The good Lord taught that boy how to do just about everything he himself knew how to do, and they did everything together almost! (The reason I said just about is because of Mark 13:32, "But of that day and that hour knoweth no man, no, neither the Son, but the Father.") The reason I said did almost everything together is because of Matthew 27:46, "And about the ninth hour Jesus cried with a loud voice, saying, E-li, E-li, la'-ma sa-bach'-tha-ni? That is to say, My God, My God, why hast thou forsaken me?) He even went ahead and taught him how to deliver his own baby brother, whom they named Adam!*

In my own mind I see Adam, Jehovah and Jesus doing many things together before little Adam had to be placed on his own path. Then came the moment when Adam was placed on his own path. Adam was quite fully developed for his age, given the short period of time that he had been on his path. He was also amazingly intelligent. He had a sense of right and wrong, but unlike his oldest brother Jesus, whom he had no memory of while on his own individual path, he was simply too young to understand the DEAD seriousness of doing wrong. He did not understand that the world he was in, was actually somewhere inside another world. And in that world if you did wrong you were put to death in a way that is beyond imagination! The only way to escape such a penalty is if someone who is not guilty of doing wrong by the same rules as the one who did wrong, volunteers to die in their place. This was the law of a land that Adam didn't even know he was living in. Whether any other of little Adam's brothers offered to do what would have to be done to rescue him, I do not know. I do know, however, that it was determined that there was only one out an unbelievable number of brothers who was actually strong enough to do it.

He would have to leave the world that he was in, enter the world where little Adam was, be born again, live 33 years without ever sinning, be beaten, tortured to death, and then burn in the fires of hell. None of this was going to be easy, but the fires of hell was (and is) something that made every Angel in heaven wonder could they do it, except for one.

The biblical account of that moment is Revelation 5:1-9, 1 "And I saw in the right hand of him that sat on the throne a book written within and on the backside, sealed with seven seals." (This is the assignment to save little Adam in the Lord's right hand.) 2 "And I saw a strong angel proclaiming with a loud voice, Who is worthy to open the book, and to lose the seals thereof? 3 And no man in heaven, or in earth, neither under the earth, was able to open the book, neither to look thereon. 4 And I wept much, because no man was found worthy to open and to read the book, neither to look thereon." (This is little Adam weeping for help) 5 "And one of the elders saith unto me, Weep not: behold, the Lion of the tribe of Juda, the root of David, hath prevailed to open the book, and to lose the seven seals thereof. 6 And I beheld, and lo, in the midst of the throne and of the four beasts, and the midst of the elders, stood a lamb as it had been slain, having seven horns and seven eyes, which are the seven spirits of God sent forth into all the earth. 7 And he came and took the book out of the right hand of him that sat upon the throne. 8 And when he had taken the book, the four beast and four and twenty elders fell down before the Lamb, having every one of them harps, and golden vials full of odours, which are the prayers of saints. 9 And they sung a new song, saying, Thou art worthy to take the book, and to open the seals thereof: for thou wast slain, and hast redeemed us to God by thy blood out of every kindred, and tongue, and people, and nation;"

(This is Jesus as he is taking little Adam's place and sending (him/us) home to (his/our daddy!)(Abba)- The word Abba is an Aramaic word that would most closely be translated as "Daddy. "It was a common term that young children would use to address their fathers. It signifies the close, intimate relationship of a father to his child, as well as the trust that a young child puts in his "Daddy."

When I say that Jesus went on this mission for the sole purpose of saving Adam, I do not mean that this is what he did symbolically. I mean that he did it literally. In the KJV Genesis 5:2 God intentionally called two people one name. Adam! "Male and female created he them: and blessed them, and called their name Adam, in the day when they were created." He did not call their names with an s. Instead he said their name. Single, meaning only one name for two people. The words mankind or man are not names. When a child is born the first thing done is it is given a name. The name is who the child is, not what the child is. Male and female is what the child became. Adam is who became male and female. Another way of saying it would be Adam divided himself into two pieces. Only Adam wasn't the one who did the dividing. Not long after Adam divided into male and female, he disobeyed and had to be put to death, even though he did not fully understand what he had done.

Then God the father said that because of the good that is in Adam, one of you, his brothers, must go and save him. Then Jesus came forward and said he is my *little brother and I will go. Remember, God the father sent Jesus to save Adam for the sake of the good that was in him, not for the sake of the evil that was in him! The good that was in Adam took the time to walk and to talk to his big brother and got to know him. Because he fully understood why his big brother did that for him, it had a profound effect on the rest of his life. 1st Corinthians 15:45 states, "And so it is written, The first man Adam was made a living soul; the last Adam was made a quickening spirit."*

Now first, we have to grasp the understanding that all of this took place before the foundation of the world! 1st Peter 1:20, "Who verily was foreordained before the foundation of the world, but was manifest in these last times for you."

I covered this in chapter 3 also, but for the sake of anyone reading this chapter I will explain. In Genesis 1:3, it says that God said let there be light. This light was Jesus. He was made to be the light of the world before anything else was done because the spiritual light that men walk in was first on God's list of priorities. The physical light that men see by was created on the fourth day in Genesis 1:14-19. Verse 3 uses the word LIGHT-S; so it is single= one light! Verses 14&15 uses the word LIGHTS, meaning more than one light. Jesus existed before the world existed, but he was not the light of the world. He had to be made the light of the world. When Jesus saved little Adam's life, he became the light that the good in Adam walked in. This was done before the world was created. Because for God's master plan to be a success from the beginning, the elements needed to guarantee success would have to already be included. Jesus saving the good in Adam was the element that guaranteed success. So it had to have happened before the first or second Adam was made flesh, and definitely before the foundation of the earth!

When God says that something has already happened, we understand it to mean that He is saying that He has already planned for it to happen. What mankind does not understand about God is that the way that God plans to do something is by doing it. Then when He is ready for us to see it, He shows it to us. If He decides to tell us about it before He causes it to appear, He will say, "Barack Obama, I have made you president of the most powerful nation in the world." Then Barack would say, "I am only 17, I can't even spell Harvard, and Lord, in case you haven't noticed I'm a little on the dark side." So the reason He speaks of things which are not as though they were, is because they are.

Many of us Christians seem to think that Jesus's mission was all about us, but it was not; although we were included. Remember, it says the Jew first then the

Gentiles. Many Jews seem to think the Messiah's mission was all about them, but it was not; although they were included. Adam is the, not one, but two, who cried out and that is when God the father made it his mission to send Jesus on a mission. Little Adam cried out when he realized he was never going to see his daddy again. This literally took place in Revelation 5:4, "And I wept much………….." The Bible experts may say that the man who made the statement "And I wept much" was John on the Island of Patmos, but where he went and what he saw, was long before he was born. In fact, it was at a time, according to the vision, when the decision was being made as to who was going to save Adam for the sake of the good that was still in him. I'm not saying John did not feel compelled to weep and indeed wept. But I am saying that he wept from within Adam. This, too, was before the foundation of the world.

Ecclesiastes 1:9, "The thing that hath been, is that which shall be; and that which is done is that which shall be done: and there is no new thing under the sun." (The thing that God has already caused to be before the world began is that which shall be; and when we see it for the first time we will say, "I know for a fact that this is brand new," but it is not!)

Now comes the scenario. Let's say you save the lives of a man and his wife by pulling their unconscious *bodies out of a burning car, and go about your way. Then 20 years later you go to see them and they have 12 children, whereas they had none when you saved them. Question: how many lives did you save, 2 or 14. Answer: 14. Likewise when the second Adam pulled the first Adam from the fire shortly after he became male and female, well you do the math. But know this, if you now see yourself as a piece of Adam, you are getting closer to the truth. You see the truth is, was and will always be what God says the truth is, and God says that you are Adam. When Adam was in one piece, God called him Adam. When Adam was in two pieces God still called him Adam. Now do you think that when Adam became three pieces that God stopped calling him Adam? Answer, no He did not. Once again you do the math!*

It is sad to say that most of us have not, nor will we ever reach the point where the death of Jesus will have a profound effect on the remainder of or lives. If we reach that point, we no longer take sin lightly at all. Not because we are afraid of dying in our sin. But because we have somehow decided to experiment for ourselves, and see if it is possible to get to know Jesus the way very few have come to know God the father. We may not admit it, but most of us talk to God the father all throughout the day, off-and-on, but only mention Jesus's name at the end of a prayer when we say, "In Jesus name we pray."

For many of us, if we communicated with God the Son the same way we communicate with God the Father, then on that faithful day we would not have to hear Jesus say to us, Matthew 7:23, "And then will I profess unto them, I never knew you: depart from me, ye that work iniquity."

We talk to God and tell him why we are going to sin, and why we already sinned. We feel the need to explain why as though it makes a difference to him, but the reality is it makes a difference only to us. The thing we fail to understand is God the father did not die on the cross, nor burn in the fires of hell for the sin you say you are about to commit or the one you already committed.

So if we feel the need to explain, then we need to explain to the one who is either going to have to go to the cross again for the sin you already committed, or will have to go through it all again for the one you say you are going to commit. When you do this, you will find that your conversation with him about the one you have already committed will have an effect upon you that you never thought possible. You see, in that conversation, he will assure you that he will do again what it takes to get you the forgiveness you need. Then he will explain what he will have to suffer in order to get you the forgiveness you must have for that one sin that you already committed. This conversation will not have to be re-

peated some ridiculous amount of times before his death begins to have what I call the profound effect, on the remainder of your life.

The main reason is this: After talking with him for a little while every time these situations come up, you won't be able to help but get to know him. When you get to know him and some of the things he has gone through in his life, then it will become increasingly harder for you do any of the things that caused the person you have gotten to know so much pain! Hebrews 6:6, "If they shall fall away, to renew them again unto repentance; seeing they crucify to themselves the Son of God afresh, and put him to an open shame." (To fall away does not mean to stop believing in Christ. To fall away means to withdraw from or become incompliant to a set of rules or expectations after having once agreed to, whether it be temporarily or permanently. So to put Hebrews 6: 6 in simple terms, it means every time you knowingly sin as a Christian, you personally cause Christ to have to make a decision to either turn you over to a reprobate mind or die on the cross again in order to free you again from the penalty of your latest sin, or sins.

At the beginning of this chapter I talked about punishment being correction and penalty being that which includes death. Jesus received both punishment and penalty. This was no coincidence. There is significance. In those times no one received both, but this was done of the father to signify that the penalty, which is his death, must be accompanied by punishment, which is the correction we receive. Correction is the definition of healing. This is why the scripture states in 1st Peter 2:24, "… … … … … … .BY HIS STRIPES YE WERE HEALED."

The other reason is this; forgiveness does not take place until we repent, and then ask for it. Now in our minds we think that what happens next is Jesus's blood is released from somewhere, and it washes away that sin, and we are in good shape. That is not what happens. It is not the blood that frees you from the death penalty that your sin, not anyone else's sin, but your sin requires take place. The death and the burning in hell fire of Christ is what frees you from the death and fire penalty. One sin, one death, but two or more sins require two or more deaths! Unless you take the risk of carrying a number of sins to bring to him and ask they be forgiven at one confession with him. Christ died more than 2,000 years ago to clear the sins of those who believed he was coming, believed he was there as they looked at him with their own eyes and those that would after his death believe that he had come and risen. That death combined with your belief caused you to be born again. Since you've been born again, he has had to return to the cross as many times as you have asked him to. This he does literally, not figuratively, as the enemy would have you believe.

The enemy tells you that it does not hurt Christ anymore. Every time you burn your hand, does it hurt, or did it hurt the first time only? When we return to sin, we return to the dark hole we were in before Christ came to our rescue. This also returns Christ to where he was before he did what it took to get you out of the dark hole the first time. He himself was not in a dark hole before he rescued you the first time. He was on safe ground. He left safe ground to crawl down into a dark hole to rescue you. So if you decide to leave safe ground and fall into that same hole again, then he will have to go through the same procedure again in order to get you to safe ground again.

This is between yourself and him. If your brother or sister does not return to that dark hole, then he does not have to go in and get them out and return to safe ground. This why Paul said in Hebrews 6:6 "unto themselves" this means as far as you and Christ are concerned, not anyone else. In other words, he is not going to allow your conscience to rest in the assumption that the work involved with rescuing you has already been established. Instead, he is allowing your conscience to rest in the assurance that the METHOD involved with *rescuing you from the dark hole has already been established! One is an assumption and the other is an assurance. As far as the world is concerned it was needed and it was done. But as far as you are concerned, if you need it to be done, then he will do it for you. The profound effect should be the fact that you fully understand what He did for you, along with the fact that you feel his pain when he almost begged the father to allow him to do it some other way, and in all truth he is almost begging you to not put him through it again, but nevertheless if you need him to he will.*

The mystery of God the Father, Son and Holy Spirit is the sequence in which they do things. We as humans do not understand how something we understand to have already happened and are over with can be something that is going to happen or be something that is happening. We have an understanding of what is possible and what is impossible. Most of the things we do not understand we rule to be impossible. The answer to this mystery is hidden in these two scriptures: the first one is the 2nd half of Exodus 3:14 "……..and he said, Thus shalt thou say unto the children of Israel, I AM hath sent me unto you." The second is in John 8:58, "Jesus said unto them, Verily, I say unto you, Before Abraham was, I am." These statements are indirect announcements of their ability to arrange and rearrange sequences involving themselves and mankind in heaven as well *as on or inside the earth. In other words, their ability to cause it to be true that they have already finished, not yet even started on and in the process of finishing the rescue of mankind simultaneously!*

Some will say, "If he already died for my sin 2,000 years ago, how can he die again for a sin I might commit tomorrow? Please explain. Answer. The thing that he has finished is the thing that he has not yet started on and the thing that he has not yet started on is the thing that he has been working on all along! This is only the beginning of the understanding that, "With him all things are possible!"

Chapter 14

What makes Patience so Valuable?

First of all, there is very little or nothing at all that the Lord can do with an impatient man or woman. There are so many things in this sample of life that hinge upon patience. If you study the Bible on a regular basis, you will notice that it seems like the Bible just can't say enough about the value of patience. In fact the scriptures appear to reverence the word patience.

The ability to continue to work toward, while waiting on a desired object, no matter how long it takes is a trait that for all practical purposes, seems to be mandatory for all Christians. First let me just say that almost every sin committed in this world in one way or another was conceived and born out of a lack of patience. Take for example fornication. It is the number one sin in the world because people can't wait to get married. Stealing, people steal because they can't wait for the Lord to provide whatever it is that they either want or need.

Cheating, people cheat to get ahead because they can't wait to get ahead the proper way.

Hebrews 10:36 states, "For ye have need of patience, that, after ye have done the will of God, ye might receive the promise." But no one in the Bible makes more clearly, the value of patience than Jesus himself. Luke 21:19 states, "In your patience possess ye your souls."

You may ask the question, "Just exactly what does that mean?" The answer goes like this. Patience is a kind of spiritual container designed to keep and preserve your Soul from the lake of fire! If you do not have patience, then that means that you do not have any kind of way of keeping and preserving your soul.

In Hebrews 11:6 it states, "But without faith it is impossible to please him: for he that cometh to God must believe that he is, and that he is a rewarder of them that diligently seek him." If the Lord where to instantly give us the things that we ask for, we would only develop short-term faith. With short term faith you do have the ability to trust the Lord, but only for a little while. This is acceptable in a new Christian, but unacceptable in a person who has been a Christian for years. It is the weakest stage of your faith.

In James 2:26 it states, "For as the body without the spirit is dead, so faith without works is dead also." Now I said that to say this; Faith without any patience at all is not faith at all! Faith with very little patience is very little faith. But faith with long-term patience is a strong, healthy and well developed faith, which pleases God. When we ask the Lord for anything in Jesus's name the scripture says that he hears us. 1st John 5:14&15 states, 14 "And this is the confidence that we have in him, that, if we ask any thing according to his will, he heareth us: 15 And if we know that he hear us, whatsoever we ask, we know that we have the petition that we desire of him."

Many times when we ask the Lord for things He intentionally takes a long time before He gives you whatever it is that you desire from him. He could give it to you quickly, but many times He takes a long time getting it to you so that he can build and strengthen your patience. He knows that patience is the number one ingredient in faith.

If the truth be told, far too many of us Christians say, "We are walking in faith," while they wait for the Lord to answer their request. But what we really do is swing back and forward; believing one day and the next day doubting because it's taking so long. And when the Lord actually gives us the very thing we ask for, we are totally surprised. Now the question of the matter is this; If we had faith that the Lord was going to give it to us, then why are we so surprised when he finally gives it to us?

There is a period of time in which the Lord delights himself above all other. That time is when one of his children asks him for something and immediately begins enjoying themselves walking in total expectation of receiving from the Lord the desired object that they requested, no matter how long they have to wait! No child of God will ever put that kind of smile on the Lord's face without patience.

Those of us who have patience will wait along beside the Lord and help him finish the work that he has started. Those of us who do not have patience will leave the Lord by himself to finish the work. We do that because we can't wait to live-it-up. Can't wait to party. Can't wait to play the games that grownups play. Can't wait to celebrate what we think is LIFE!

But what we do not know is that the Lord himself, including the entire host of heaven is eagerly waiting to celebrate true life with us. They have placed their own life on hold; working hard to build a new heaven, a place where we and they can enjoy LIFE together and never again have to worry about the clock running out of time. So to those of us on the earth who think we are the only ones who just-can't-wait to have some fun, think again!

Chapter 15

Daddy's Love

If a man and woman have a child and circumstances many years later dictate that they must take the child's life in self-defense, a child that they loved with all their heart and soul: Question. Does the love that the parents had for their child diminish at all just because they had to put the child down? Answer. No it does not. Nothing can separate the child from the love of its parents.

The lord loves all of his children and even Satan is a child of God, due to the fact that he did not create himself. Even though the lord has to cast him into the lake of fire in the end, he still loves him. The same thing goes for those of us whom the lord will not allow to enter into the kingdom on judgment day. Those of us who will not be allowed to enter the Kingdom will be no different than Satan! Romans 8:38&39 states, 38 "For I am persuaded, that neither death, nor life, nor angels, nor principalities, nor powers, nor, things present, nor things to come, 39 nor height, nor depth, nor any other creature, shall be able to separate us from the love of God, which is in Christ Jesus our Lord."

In my opinion I do not think that it is possible for man to come close to comprehending the Love that the Father, the Son and the Holy Spirit has for us. There are three verses in the Bible that I have known for years that I would quote when I got to this part of this book. But it wasn't until I actually got to the point where I was about to write them down, that I began to start feeling the magnitude of his concern for us. Matthew 10:29-31 states, 29 "Are not two sparrows sold for a farthing? And one of them shall not fall on the ground without your Father. 30 But the very hairs of your head are all numbered. 31 Fear ye not therefore, ye are of more value than many sparrows."

There is a sad truth in this world we live in and that sad truth is this; you can come to understand to some degree, how much another person loves you, but for some reason you cannot feel how much they love you. The chance to love and be loved is the greatest gift that life has to offer. I have a fear for the people whom I love dearly. This fear cannot be described with words alone. I love the Lord and my fear for him is the pain he will suffer when all of his children do not make it back home. In Matthew 10:30, the Lord is not trying to make *you understand that he loves you. Most of us deep down inside, either knows or believes that he does love us.*

What the Lord is trying to do in Matthew 10:30, is to make you understand the magnitude of his love for you. I personally do not know why we as human beings do not possess the capacity to feel how much another person loves us, but I do know this; we as human beings have a limited capacity when it comes to handling emotions.

Whether they are positive or negative, it does not matter. Sometimes we get so filled with joy that we can't hold back the tears. Sometimes we are so filled with so much sadness that the same thing happens and once again we cannot hold back the tears. It is for these two reasons I am totally convinced that if any human being were to somehow feel the magnitude of the love that God has for them it would be far too much for them to handle. It would most likely result in their own death! Another thing I would like to expound upon is the fact that there are many books, classified as NEAR DEATH EXPERIENCES. These are basically testimonies people of every race, color and creed have written to declare what they experienced during the short period of time in which they were declared legally dead.

What all of them have in common was the fact that when they felt or were somehow informed that it was time for them to leave the place where they were, they became almost hysterical in their intent on not leaving this place that they had found themselves in. None of them had actually seen God, but they could feel a presence that they could not describe and all they knew was they never wanted to leave that feeling. What these people may or may not know is the fact that what they were feeling was in fact the love that is inside God! His love is so dense that they could feel it. Ironically enough, this is the same love that if a live human being could feel it would kill them.

The reason they could feel it and live to tell the story is because they were already clinically dead at the time they experienced it. But it is possible for us to somewhat begin to understand it. That is the purpose for Matthew 10:30. It is to hopefully cause you to begin to understand the magnitude of his love for you.

Let us begin with the fact that Jesus has never committed a sin in his life. If he has never sinned, then that means he has never told a lie. If he never told a lie, then that means he was telling the truth when he said that the Father is so consumed with his love for us that he took the time to sit down and actually count every single hair on each one of our heads! Now if you can just stop whatever you are doing for a few minutes and think about this. Who in the world could be so madly in love with you that they would take the time to sit down and count each hair on you head?

In the world that we live in; if a woman fell so in love with a man that she kept a record of each of the hairs on his head, then that man would be afraid of that woman. He would be totally convinced that she is crazy. Why? Because in this world we do not understand this kind of love. How can something so seemingly insignificant to me be so important to my heavenly Father? If he is that concerned about my hair, just imagine how concerned he must be about every other thing concerning me.

I know there are some that will say, "It makes no sense to say that simply feeling the love of God unleashed upon you could kill you."

Well to that I say that it makes no sense to say that if a man simply looks at God the Father it would result in his death! In (Exodus 33:18&20-23) it states, 18 "And he said, I beseech thee, show me thy glory." 20 "And he says, Thou canst not see my face: for there shall no man see me, and live. 21 And the Lord said, Behold, there is a place by me, and thou shalt stand upon a rock: 22 And it shall come to pass, while my glory passeth by, that I will put thee in a cleft of the rock, and will cover thee with my hand while I pass by: 23 And I will take away mine hand, and thou shalt see my back parts: but my face shall not be seen." If looking at him can do that, then know this, his love is ten times stronger than his look!

If there was a scripture in the Bible that said that God counted each of the hairs on just Jesus's head; I could understand that. But why would he do something like that for me?

Chapter 16

Voices in my Head

In (Genesis 3:22) it states, "And the Lord God said, Behold, the man is become as one of us, to know good and evil:… … … … … … ." The statement is and was true, but what does it mean? There are many who would say, "It is a self-explanatory statement, and it doesn't need to be explained." The truth is they could never be further from the truth if they think that the first half of (Genesis 3:22) does not need to be explained.

Let me start by first saying that there was a time when I also thought there was no explanation needed for this particular verse other than the surface explanation. But the time came when the Holy Spirit was ready to reveal to us what was beneath the surface. When the good Lord spoke in the first half of (Genesis 3:22) and said, "Behold, the man is become as one of us, to know good and evil:" He was not saying that man had acquired exactly what he himself, the Son and all of the angels had pertaining to the knowledge of good and evil. This is the place where everyone gets thrown off because a very complex statement was made without the benefit of explanation.

With that having been said, I will now say it the way he meant it. I am not making an attempt to correct the Lord God All Mighty. I am not saying "this nor that" is what the Lord meant to say. I am simply saying this is what he meant when he said what he said. What he meant was man, for all practical purposes has acquired virtually the same ability we have when it comes to the knowledge of good and evil; although not the exact same thing.

The difference between what God, Jesus and the angels have concerning knowledge of good and evil and that which mankind has is this. God, Jesus and the angels have celestial/invisible bodies which they live in alone by their individual selves. It is each one's individual temple.

When they think upon a situation in order to decide whether or not to do the right thing, they listen to themselves think. So the voice they hear inside their head whenever they are thinking is and always has been their own internal voice.

Mankind on the other hand, has a terrestrial/fleshly visible body. Our bodies are our temples that we live in.

We are invisible, but the body we live in is not. From the very beginning of our life on this earth we are not alone in this individual temple that each of us live inside. There is a minimum of two other invisible beings like ourselves living in our temple with each of us.

When we think upon a situation in order to decide whether to do the right thing; we do not listen to ourselves in thought. The voice we hear inside our head whenever we are thinking is not our own internal voice 90% of the time. Less than 10% of the time it is our own internal voice. But the longer we live the percentage of time in which we listen to our own internal voice will slowly but surely increase.

How much it increases is difficult to say because it depends entirely on each individual person. Of the two voices that we hear, one is the knowledge of good and the other the knowledge of evil. But know this; neither of the two are wasting their time. One of them is teaching us how to think good and do good. The other is teaching us how to think evil and do evil.

Literally speaking, mankind borrows these other two beings to be used as our very own knowledge of good and our very own knowledge of evil. When our creators created us they intentionally left that part out. One of the reasons why they did that can be found in (Ezekiel

28:15) and it reads, "Thou wast perfect in thy ways from the day that thou wast created, till iniquity was found in thee." Iniquity is not something that is created by God the father, but rather something that is formulated by the children of God. It originates from their own inherited creative nature whether it is man or angel.

The knowledge of evil, which is an unclean spirit, acts as if it is our own internal evil voice while teaching us how to become what it is all along. The knowledge of good, which is a clean spirit, act as our own internal good voice while teaching us how to become what it is all along. So you see by the time a human being dies, he or she will have developed within themselves something that they were convinced that they had from birth, which is their own knowledge of good and evil.

So there is no such thing as an evil nature, nor is there any such thing as a sinful nature. We are born with a knowledge of good and a knowledge of evil living inside our bodies with us, but they are not our own! (The voices in my head are not my own, but some day they will be!) We are slowly developing the ability to think, without the aid of the voice of the knowledge of good nor the aid of the voice of the knowledge of evil.

If mankind developed a method of determining whether a child is going to be a violent criminal or a law *abiding citizen while the baby was still in the fetus stage of development; then they would abort all of the ones that are destined to be violent criminals. Then allow the ones that are destined to become law abiding citizens to be born into this world. We will never fully develop this ability while living in the flesh. But we will develop it enough for the Lord to make a decision as to whether or not to allow us to live in the world that he lives in!*

Chapter 17

From Earth to Heaven, How Far?

Mankind has always perceived heaven to be a place far, far away from here where we are on planet earth. We picture scriptures in our mind like (Acts 1:9) where it states, "And when he had spoken these things, while they beheld, he was taken up; and a cloud received him out of their sight." And in (Colossians 3:2) "Set your affection on things above, not on things on the earth."

First I want to say that I am not trying to add anything to, nor take anything away from the Bible. What I am trying to do is give a more realistic geographic view of where we are, and where Heaven is. And most importantly where God is. Consider this:

(There are three worlds. The first world is inside the second world, and the second world is inside the third world.) We start with hell itself. Hell is a world. In (Isaiah 5:14) it states, "Therefore hell hath enlarged herself, and opened her mouth without measure: and their glory, and their multitude, and their pomp, and he that rejoiceth, shall descend into it." Hell is totally surrounded by the earth. If you were in hell, whatever direction you point, you would be pointing at the earth.

The earth is also a world and it is totally surrounded by Heaven itself! Heaven also is a world. Our terminology for directions is what keeps us from clearly understanding exactly where we are. Up is not really up; actually a more accurate description of up would be the word (outward); and down is not really down. A more accurate description would be (inward). In the back of our mind we somehow think that if it were possible for us to live long enough, that we could get into a spaceship, and travel far enough to actually reach heaven. What I am saying is that whenever the thought or conversation about heaven pops up, we automatically think of whatever way we visualize it to be, along with the thought of distance. Ironically, it is this universal acceptance of an undetermined distance from earth to heaven, which keeps us from realizing exactly where we are.

If you take 1,000 men and placed them at equal distances apart over the face of the earth and the seas, and commanded them all to point at heaven at the same time, you would find that because the earth is made like a round ball, they would all be pointing outward in a thousand different directions. This is looking at the world from the big picture.

But if you were to ask each one what direction he's pointing; each would say they are pointing up. This is looking at the world from the small picture.

My point is this: If I were to unknowingly go into the Superdome in New Orleans, and walk to the middle of the football field blindfolded, and start pointing in every direction I can think of, and wherever I point, someone told me that I was pointing at the superdome. At that point I would have to conclude that due to the fact that wherever I point, I am still pointing at the superdome, and then I have to be inside the superdome! Now at that point it would be unfitting for me to say that "I am going to go to the superdome." Because even though I am blindfolded and can't see it; I would already know that I am already in it!

Now I said all that to say this; If we the people on earth, point in every direction we find that no matter where we point, we are still pointing at heaven. So we have no choice but to conclude that the only way for heaven to totally surround the earth –all sides, top and bottom– is for the earth to be located right in the middle of heaven itself. So when we think about going to heaven, remember that geographically speaking, we are on a planet that is already there! In other words we are basically located in the good Lord's front living room. Literally! When we were little children, we were taught that God was way-way up there and we are way down here. It is this illusion of some type of great distance that somehow encourages us to participate in all manner of sin and abominations.

Each of us in our own way, at some point began experimenting with what we had been told about God. God was different from Santa Claus, the Boogie-Man, or the Good Tooth Ferry. Big-Momma talked about him all the time, and every time we went down to Big-Momma's house, she made everybody in the house go to church on Sundays to talk about God. She even made my Daddy and Momma go!

She was the one who got me interested in God when I was about three years old. Then one night my daddy taught me how to talk to Him for the first time. I will never forget it. Daddy had on his T-shirt and shorts and I did too, and he said, "OK, you get down on your knees, and put your hands together, lean on the bed, close your eyes and say this here; "Now I lay me down to sleep"---and I said---"now I lay me down to sleep," and he said, I pray to God my soul to keep---and I said---"I pray to God my soul to keep", and he said, if I should die before

I awake---and I said---"*if I should die before I awake*" and he said, *I pray to God my soul to take*---and I said---"*I pray to God my soul to take*" and he said, *Amen*---and I said---"*Amen*"!

It was Big-Momma who explained to me how God works when I was almost three years old. (My memory goes back to before I was one year old; but that's another long story.) Anyway, she told me about how a man borrowed some money from her and did not pay her back, and how the Lord punished him. Then, I suppose, because I was such a naughty little child, she explained how the lord punishes little boys when they are bad. She said when you do something bad, and momma or daddy finds out about it, then you will get a whipping: But if you do something bad and momma-nem don't know nothin' about what you did, that don't mean that you got away with it. Because the Good Lord seen you do it and if momma-nem don't ever find out about it, then the Good Lord himself will give you a whippin'.

To be honest, I don't remember why she went on to tell me how the Good Lord gives naughty little bad boys a whippin, but it could not have been the look on my face that said she had my undivided attention when she said God can give you a whippin, Because Big-Momma was almost completely blind. I might have asked her how does he go about givin me a whippin? I remember her saying "Well, he does different ways, like you might get your finger caught in the screen door, that be the Lord spankin' you for doing something that you an't had no business doing, or you might get stung by a honey bee."

Now here is the part that reminded me of every word she said, and made a believer out of a little knuckle-headed boy. I remember one time I was at Big-Momma's and I got a my hands on a B-B-gun and went down to the hog pen. I was shooting the pigs and nobody knew about it even to this day, but I think uncle Shyann suspected it was me. One night around that time my uncles were going to the store. Big-Momma always would make them take me too. Plus she would give me some pocket money. I got in the back seat and for some reason I left my hand in car door way too long. My uncle closed the door on my hand and I cried and cried. It seems like to me that I can remember someone in the car saying to me after they saw I was OK, and my fingers weren't broken, "That's what you get for being so bad, the Good Lord don't like ugliness!"

Another time I got the same B-B gun and I was under the house shooting the chickens. I thought I had gotten away with that too. However, a little time later I picked up a plastic baseball in Big-Momma's front yard. A honey bee was in it and the bee stung me. Nobody had to say it that time, cause I remembered, The Good Lord don't like ugliness.

Now I said all that to make this point: ever since those days as a little boy, I believed that He was up there in heaven, and He eventually would get around to doing something about the things I do that he does not like. Yet not being able to see him nor anyone else at the point in which I was about to commit sin, somehow contributed in a way I cannot describe.

I felt that although the Lord had supernatural eyesight, still there was this great distance between me and what I was doing and his eyes with their supernatural ability. So I took a kind of comfort in my perceived distance between us. This made sinning feel somewhat more comfortable. Even the scriptures seem to indicate distance. Matthew 25:14 states, "For the kingdom of heaven is as a man travelling into a far country, who called his own servants, and delivered unto them his goods." That being said, I now say you cannot imagine how shocked I was when the Holy Spirit began removing the scales from my eyes and thereby revealing to me for the first time, the true geographical location of the invisible living God.

All of my life I had always focused on the distance that He and I were apart. I never ever focused on how close He would had to have been, to be able to hear my voice when I whispered a prayer to him in all, not just some, of my emergency situations. The Holy Spirit pointed out to me, just how close I had to be to another person for them to hear what I am saying without me having to shout.

The Holy Spirit also reminded me that people I talk to on a daily basis are just as invisible as God himself; If not for the fact they are woven into the flesh they live in. They could be standing right in front of you, face to face and you would never know they were there, because you would be looking right through them.

Remember, we can't even see ourselves. Everyone on earth thinks that what they see in the mirror is what they look like, when what they see in the mirror is what their flesh looks like. There is a scripture that's a perfect example of the revelation I am trying to convey.

Elisha, the man of God, was surrounded by enemy soldiers. His servant was afraid and asked Elisha, "What will we do?" The servant asked that question because he had a set of standard issue human eyes. He could not see the huge host of angles in chariots of fire, gathered around them to protect them. Elisha's servant could not see the angels, because he was looking right through them as though they were not there at all. That is, until the Lord opened his eyes also. (2nd Kings 6:14-17) states, 14 *"Therefore sent he thither horses, and chariots, and a great host: and they came by night, and compassed the city about. 15 And when the servant of the man of God was risen early, and gone forth, behold, a host compassed the city both with horses and chariots. And his servant said unto him, Alas, my master! How shall we do? 16 And he answered, fear not: for they that be with us are more than they that be with them. 17 And Elisha prayed, and said, Lord, I pray the open his eyes, that he may see. And the Lord opens the eyes of the young man; and he saw: and, behold, the mountain was full of horses and chariots of fire round about Elisha."*

The definition for the word heaven is open space from the ground to the clouds, and also from the clouds to what we call outer space. So when we look at the clouds, what we are really doing is, looking through heaven in order to gaze at the clouds and when skies are clear, even beyond. Remember, the empty space is called heaven. (Genesis 1:6-8) states, 6 *"And God said, Let there be a firmament, in the midst of the waters, and let it divide the waters from the waters. 7 And God made the firmament, and divided the waters which were under the firmament from the waters which were above the firmament: and it was so. 8 And God called the firmament heaven. And the evening and the morning were the second day."*

In other words, God lifted what we would call fog, from lying on the body of water, put it in the sky, and the open, empty, invisible, sometimes clear, see-through space between them, he named heaven. Some people like to categorize it as the first, second and third heaven. But on a day or a night when there isn't a cloud in the sky, which means there are no clouds to divide the so-called first heaven from the second heaven! And by the way: what does the lord use to keep the third and the second heaven divided from each other? Because God forbid should they become tangled up!

I am not trying to make fun of what little knowledge mankind has of the heavens. The spirit of the Lord has not called me to make fun of the knowledge that we have. He has called me, and given me understanding and instructed me to add that understanding to the knowledge we already have! (Proverbs 4:7) states "Wisdom is the principal thing; therefore get wisdom: and with all thy getting get understanding." In 2 Corinthians 12:1-4 Paul describes a vision that he experienced in which he was called up to the third heaven. He also states that he does not know whether he was in his body in the vision or if his spirit was the only part of him that went. What he means by that is he did not see his own hand or foot or any part of his own body during the vision, so he doesn't know whether he was wearing his flesh so-to-speak at the time or not.

The reason that I know is because I was, I guess you could say, caught up to heaven in a vision also, but I heard no words. I was at a level where only a little more than my shoulders were slightly above what seemed to be clouds. A whitish- grayish horse walked in front of me, very close to me and stood there for maybe 30 seconds. I was facing its side and saw no one on the horse at the time, (but found out more than six years later that there was someone on that horse!) Then suddenly, the vision was over! But I had not noticed whether I could see my hands or feet or any part of my flesh. Yet when Paul mentioned that one little detail, it reminded me that I do not recall seeing any part of my flesh during my vision either.

Now don't think for a second that I wish to be placed in any sort of rank as Paul. But I do know what he meant. (2nd Corinthians 12:1-4) states 1 " It is not expedient for me doubtless to glory, I will come to visions and revelations of the lord. 2 I knew a man in Christ above fourteens year ago, (whether in the body, I cannot tell; or whether out of the body, I cannot tell; God knoweth;) such an one caught up to the third heaven. 3 And I knew such a man, (whether in body or out of body, I cannot tell; God knoweth;) 4 How that he was *caught up into paradise, and heard unspeakable words, which is not for a man to utter."*

The main point is this: empty, clear, see through, invisible space starts at less than one inch off the ground, and continues outward, further than any man can travel, even if we still had the ability to live 969 years, like Methuselah. Not only that, but you can hold your arm strait out in front of you, with the back of your hand facing you, and guess what? From the tip of your nose to the back of your hand, there is nothing but, empty, clear, see through, invisible space.

There is such a thing as truth, but there is also such a thing as a deeper truth, and the deepest truth is that we live in an invisible world that has more than enough visible things in it to thoroughly convince us that we live in a visible world where everything is visible, including the body we live in. (Even if we have just come into the knowledge that we are invisible beings, living inside visible bodies, that the old fashion Bible calls a temple!)

By now I sincerely hope a picture is starting to emerge. If so, good, because we have a little bit more to go. I have lived my whole life under the illusion that you have to go up-up-up to get to heaven. So when I had the vision, I was in that particular frame of mind.

In my vision I was walking along a road, and a big dog came running after me. It looked like he was about to get me. So I willed myself to levitate off the ground. This is something I have found that I seem to be able to do in most of my dreams or visions. As I was levitating up out of the dog's reach, I noticed I was coming up to, then passing, and looking down at a post with electrical wires.

At that point I remember being afraid for a second because I never levitated this far, but something gave me the idea to go higher. Not necessarily to try to go to heaven, but maybe—I don't know, just go-I hope I don't fall from this far up---suddenly I was in a still place that looked like I was from my waist up in what appeared to be a cloud and a horse walked in front of me.

When I used to think back on the vision, which by now was more than 12 years ago when it occurred, but over 6 years ago when I found out that there was someone on the horse.

I always assumed that I popped up through the cloud. But as I began to write this book, the Lord slowed everything down concerning the vision. This allowed me to see something you would think would not make that much of a difference, but after He showed it to me, it made a world of difference.

He showed me that my will to make the effort to travel toward where I perceived heaven to be, was his doing. He did it that way because of my frame of mind as to where heaven was in my way of thinking at that time. I did not pop through a cloud and see the things that I saw. My mindset was that I am going someplace, and while I was still in the process going someplace, I was suddenly there. I was traveling through the invisible and suddenly the visible appeared. What I saw simply appeared. When I say appeared, I mean I did not go to it and look at it. Although I was trying to do just that. Like when Jesus appeared out of thin air in (Luke 24:15&37-39) 15 "And it came to pass, that while they communed together and reasoned, Jesus himself drew near, and went with them. 37 But they were terrified and affrighted. And supposed that they had seen a spirit. 38 And he said unto them, why are ye troubled? And why do thoughts arise in your hearts? 39 Behold my hands and my feet, that it is I myself: handle me, and see; for a spirit hath not flesh and bones, as ye see me have."

Now whether or not there is such a thing as distance in heaven is not the point that we, for our own sakes, should be concerned with. We should be concerned with the fact that after coming into the knowledge that you are not in one room, and God is in the next room, but you and God all Mighty are in the same room at all times. The bad news in all of this is that if you have read this chapter then you are no longer innocent of this fact.

So the answer to the question; what is the distance from earth to heaven? The answer is literally, from visibility to invisibility. Of which there are no such scales to measure these two.

Chapter 18

The Invisible Me

There are many things that we concern ourselves with in this world, but the number one thing that we must be concerned with is our own soul. It is not wrong in any way for a person to be concerned about his own soul first and above all else. Because if in the end you go to the lake of fire, then you will immediately become concerned with nothing or no one except your own soul! Only then it will be too late. So now is the time to make it your number one concern.

Now do not confuse what I am saying with selfishness. As a matter of fact the best way to secure your soul and keep it secure is to always put the needs of others before yourself. The Father, Son and Holy Spirit's number one concern for all of us is our souls. In other words, the "YOU" that cannot be seen. You cannot see yourself. If you stand in front of a mirror you can only take a good look at the body that you live in.

People have a tendency to not believe a thing unless they can see some proof. Well do you have the proof to confirm that YOU exist? The only thing that really matters is that you yourself know that you exist. Even though we have never seen ourselves and do not have a clue as to what we look like, we know for sure that we exist. You know what the fleshly body that belongs to "YOU" looks like, but you do not know what "YOU", the one that owns that body, looks like!

The number one problem in the world today as far as parents and children are concerned, is that the world's parents work their fingers to the bone to make sure their children are happy. Happy where at? "In this world." To make sure they get an education. Educating them about what? "This world." To make sure to they are successful. Successful where at? "In this world."

There is no doubt in my mind, that the parents of today love their children. But there is a right and a wrong way to love. They love the child they can see. And do not know what to make of the child they can't see, but both are the same. We must learn to know the child that we cannot see with our eyes as well as teach them to get to know the "YOU" that they cannot see. There are so many parents guilty of doing the things that they do for their children, not as much for their child's benefit as *much as for their own benefit. So many parents do this that it would be difficult to put a number on. You might ask, "How is that so?"*

Your life is wrapped up in your child's life and you want your child to be happy. Why? Because if your child is happy, then you are happy. What you can't see in this statement is the last four words. Those four words are, "Then you are happy"! So the bottom line is you are keeping yourself happy by keeping your child happy!

You have to be able to do the things that temporally make your child unhappy in order to keep them on the path that leads to Heaven, as well as a promising career. Notice, I did not say keep them on the path that leads them to a promising career, as well as to Heaven. Instead, I said it the other way around. This is what the Bible says about this very situation. Now the subject is chastisement, which is not what I intend to point out. What I intend to point out in this piece of scripture is what the true motive is for the fathers and mothers chastising their children. Hebrews 12:9&10 states, 9 "Furthermore we have had fathers of our flesh which corrected us, and we gave them reverence: shall we not much rather be in subjection unto the father of spirits, and live? 10. For they verily for a few days chastened us after their own pleasure; but he for our profit, that we might be partaker of his holiness."

In verse 10 it says that our parents correct us so that we will do the things that are pleasing in their own eye sight. Things that make our parents happy and things that make us happy. As parents, we tell our daughters they should use birth control and we tell our sons to use condoms. This is before they get married.

If you were to take a poll asking 100 parents what is their biggest worry when it comes to their children; only one or two would say their main concern is whether or not their child will be accepted into the kingdom of Heaven when the child dies!

No parent wants to see their child in prison and more importantly, no parent wants to go to their own child's funeral. But what the parent does not know is that when that child's spirit leaves their body, that parent will have to attend their child's FIRST funeral. The reason why is because it is the child's first death. But if the child is rejected from entering the kingdom, then the parent will also have to attend their child's second funeral, because it will be the child's second DEATH!

Then after they have witnessed their child's second death and funeral, the Lord will then wipe away all tears from their eyes! Revelation 21:4 states, "And God shall wipe away all tears from their eyes; and there shall be no more death, neither sorrow, nor crying, neither shall there be any more pain: for the former things are passed away."

I would probably die if I saw my child dead. This is with me knowing that they still stand a chance to make it to heaven. Who would I call on if I had to watch them die again? The second death. The angels would have to... ... ... !

If parents teach their children to gain the things of this world first; then worry about religion next, then that is exactly what they will do. But the scriptures say right the opposite. Matthew 6:23 states, "But seek ye first the kingdom of God, and his righteousness; and all these things shall be added unto you." Matthew 16:26 states, "For what is a man profited if he shall gain the whole world, and lose his own soul? Or what shall a man give in exchange for his soul?"

I am not saying that it is wrong for parents to love their children, nor am I saying it is wrong to do the things that they do for their children. But I am saying that if you the parent, are always concerned as to whether or not you yourself are going to be excepted into the kingdom of heaven, then you need to do everything in your power to make sure that your children are just as concerned as you are about whether or not they themselves will be excepted into the kingdom.

I say this because we, as parents, have been fortunate to live long enough to learn to seek the kingdom first. Then we turn right around and teach our own children that your career comes first. Parents who have depended on the Lord first all of their lives, but when it comes to their children, they teach them to depend on a career first! The invisible you must become your number one concern in this very visible world. Likewise, you must teach your child the same. I will not be around until the end of the world; at least I do not think so. But this book, I believe will be. So I feel the spirit leading me to explain just a little bit more about this invisibility. In other words, Proof. This proof that the spirit is leading me to explain has to be relayed in the form of a hypothetical scenario.

Let us just say that we are at a professional football game with 100,000 people in the stadium. One of the referees collapses on the field. The paramedics arrive, pick him up, place him on a scale and it shows that he weighs 186lbs. They ask him a few questions and then prepare to put him in the ambulance. Suddenly he passes out, his heart stops beating and he stops breathing. Paramedics immediately begin CPR in effort to try to revive him, but after 15 minutes with no response *they turn to the people in the stands and announce that HE IS GONE. In other words, no longer with us. Don't forget that his body is still lying on a scale and it still weighs 186lbs.*

So let just say that someone from the stands run on to the field and begs them to try just one more time. So they try again and after one more minute of CPR the man regains a pulse and even regains consciousness. So the paramedics turn around and announce to the people in the stands that HE IS BACK and with us again. Now he is still on the scale and still weighs 186lbs.

The point is this; the referee died in the middle of a football field with 100,000 witnesses. Was gone for 15 minutes and then returned. Nobody saw him leave and nobody saw him come back. If he left and returned with that many witnesses and no one seen him do it, then he is without a doubt, invisible. Just exactly like his Father which is in heaven. The eyes in your head will not allow you to see God, but don't get upset. They won't allow you to see your own self!

Chapter 19

Passing the Test

When we finally reach adulthood, get out into this world and start experiencing this thing we call Life: If we pay close attention, we will notice that it seems to be filled with two things, from beginning to end, with a very small break in between those two things.

One of the two things this so-called Life is filled with is called "Problems" and the other is called "Temptations!" The break in between has a name, which we will get to a little later in this chapter.

First, I want to say that sometimes we cannot distinguish between the two. In the heat of the moment while we are dealing with a situation that we do not yet know how to categorize, we don't know whether it is a Problem or a Temptation, or a little of both. We do know that when it comes to problems, we have to first figure out what the answer to the problem is and then apply it, in order to solve the problem. With temptation, we know we have to either figure out how to get past it, without getting too close to it, so as to not be sucked into it by its its powerful magnetic gravitational pull. Or we have to summon the strength to resist the pull of temptation as we walk directly through its gravity field. We eventually learn to resist the ones we are strong enough to resist, and AVOID the ones we are too weak to resist.

Before I go any further I will say that the Lord's overall purpose is for us to eventually reach a point where we can resist all temptations presented to us, because to do so is the essence of the word graduation. Every time we fail to solve a problem or fail to deal with temptation correctly, the same problem or temptation eventually presents itself again. Now the *irony* of it all is this: when we finally get it right, we always get a little break. But the break is always interrupted by either another problem or another temptation that just happens to be a little bit harder, or a little more complicated than the problem or temptation we dealt with before the break!

The apple of our eye, our true one desire in all of this madness, seems to be the break! The break is that small period of time in which we are not dealing with any of life's major problems nor temptations. As I said before, the brake is the place we all love to be. But one of the problems that we do not understand to even be a problem, is the break itself. We desire the break so strongly that we begin to leave problems halfway or totally un-

solved, and instead of resisting or avoiding temptations, we give in to them. All this, just to get to the break!

Usually by the time we reach this point, alcohol, drugs and/or sex, becomes our favorite refuge! And before we know it, we become refugees, fleeing from having to solve problems and from having to resist or avoid temptation. The reason alcohol, drugs and/or sex become our favorites, is because through these things we obtain immediate temporary access to the BREAK! We can take a break just by meditating on sex. Often the desire to become rich is nothing more than an effort to secure the means to turn the temporary break into a permanent break. Three things, # 1 breaks, # 2 temptations, and # 3 problems.

Earlier in this chapter I said there was a name for those breaks. The real name for those breaks is the word "recess". When we were young and in school, the thing we looked forward to the most was recess time. Recess time was a time when we didn't have to be concerned with the responsibility of solving English, math or science problems. Recess was also a time in which we did not have to deal with the pressure of taking any kind of test. Classes all day, with little recesses in between. Oh how we wished it could be recess all day, instead of class all day. From the 1st to the 6th grade, all we wanted to do was play on the swings and ride the merry-go-rounds. Then came the 7th through the 12th grade, where some of us even discovered that if we smoked a little pot/marijuana before class, that it was a way of being in class, and being on recess at the same time!

The word temptation is derived from the base or roots word tempt, which means test. So when we experience temptation, we are actually, experiencing a test! We learned to hate taking a test, and would sometimes skip school to AVOID a test. Now the *irony* of this whole going to school, solving problems in class every day, taking test thing, was; when we finally finished solving whatever math problem, or taking whatever English test the teacher gave us, we would get a small break or recess. Then once again, we would be confronted with an even harder English or math problem than before! Something else we most definitely don't want to forget about the good old school days is the fact that every time we failed to solve a problem correctly or failed a test, we would eventually wind up having to deal with it again and again until we finally got it right. Now I don't know about you, but I am starting to see a pattern emerge.

It appears that my mother and FATHER went through the trouble of putting me through 12 years of school, just to prepare me for what they used to call.... The Real World...! My daddy's name is James Henry Heard. He used to say to me all the time, "Boy, you gona see what I'm talking about when you get out here in the real world." The thought that used to always cross my mind whenever he said that was, "Daddy must not know that I'm already in the real world. I really am going to play pro-football or pro-basketball one or the other! He may be my daddy, but who does he think he is..? Accusing me of living in an imaginary world!"

Now that I am out here in what mama and daddy called, "The real world", I realize that back then I really was living in an imaginary world. The pattern that has emerged from this is, I realize that I am still in some kind of a school. Daddy is the one putting me through this school, not my earthly daddy, but my real daddy! This school is to get me prepared for real life, not a real sample of life, because thanks to the Holy Spirit's teaching, I finally realize that I am already living the sample of life. If I pass all of my tests, I will graduate to real life.

There are four categories of tests and I must get a passing grade in all four. The first is love. First of all, love has a feeling that accompanies it, but it is not a feeling. The letters L, O, V and E spell the word love, but love is not a word! Love is an action. A long time ago someone saw a person as they cared for someone else and they said to themselves, "I have to think of a name *for this combination of actions and feelings." The name that they came up with was the word "love". John 15:12 states, "This is my commandment, That ye love one another, as I loved you." The best word to describe love is the word "charity"! Charity is love in motion, or you could say charity is love in the process of actually being love! In (1st Peter 4:8) it states, "And above all things have fervent charity among yourselves: for charity shall cover the multitude of sins".*

Now to be perfectly honest, none of us Christians of today like to be reminded of the verse I am about to quote, because it reminds us of how selfish we really are. You see, the more money we have while we are still alive, the better we feel. But when we go before the throne of judgment, we will feel right the opposite. Because then the more money we will have given away when we were alive, the better we will feel then. Acts 4:34&35 states, 34"Neither was there any among them that lacked: for as many as were possessors of lands or houses sold them, and brought the prices of the things that were sold, 35 And laid them down at the apostles' feet: and distribution was made unto every man according as he had need."

Some people are not easy to love and some are. Whether or not people are easy to love or not, is not the point. The point is you need to make a passing grade in this category. It's not like you have your own life to live, right here and right now, because life does not exist in the world we now live. Remember, your real life is with Christ. You were sent here only to determine whether or not you want real life or will you settle for just a sample!

Colossians 3:2&3 states, 2 "Set your affections on things above, not on things on the earth. 3 ... .,and your life is hid with Christ in God." If you focus on what it is that you must do in order to graduate, then every time you are confronted with the perfect opportunity to hate someone, slow down, concentrate and take back all the hatred that may have already slipped out of you. Replace it with the definition of the word love.

One of the main reasons Love/Charity is so precious is for obedience sake. Sin is disobedience point-blank. Love/Charity has the ability to cover a multitude of disobedience. Obedience is one of the categories you have to pass. Sometimes you may have to wait until the next day to do it, but practice doing it on the spot, right then and there, until you get good at it. Don't confuse this with forgiveness, because we haven't gotten to that yet!

The second category is mercy. The first thing I want to say about mercy is there is no way I can say enough about how crucial mercy is to our being allowed into life *itself! In case you do not understand what mercy is or how to apply it to a situation, mercy is when you have to assert the law, or enforce a rule, and instead of administering the full punishment that the act of disobedience deserves, you have mercy on the subject, be it man or animal. You sentence the subject to only a fraction of the penalty they deserve, and in some cases, even let them go entirely. It is a simple principle, because in these situations you get to play the role of the judge. Whether you know it or not, the decisions you make at these moments will testify for you, or against you when you come before the Lord to be judged for your own disobediences.*

So you can never allow your anger to judge anyone or anything, especially your child. A parent is the one who teaches a child how to have mercy. We do not want the Lord's anger to judge our disobedience on that day. Our own hope can be seen in the eyes of the soul that rejoices over our decision to have mercy on them, be it man or be it animal! Moses used himself as a human shield to protect the children of Israel from God's anger, not from God. God himself placed Jesus between himself to sure not to allow his anger to judge us. If God, in his own own opinion, thought it best to not judge man in anger, then do you not think that man can find favor with God if he never allows his anger to judge man, beast, nor child?

So once again for obedience sake, we have to make a passing grade in the category of mercy. In James 2:12&13 states, 12 "So speak ye, and so do, as they that shall be judged by the law of liberty. 13 For he shall have judgment without mercy, that have shewed no mercy; and mercy rejoiceth against judgment." In other words, when condemnation is about to drag me into the fire, mercy will step in and save the day, Judgment-day! You will rejoice with a scream so loud that the Father, Son and the Holy Spirit will all have to take their hands and cover up their ears until you get through rejoicing!

The third one is forgiveness. One of the things we need to be aware of when it comes to forgiveness is the fact that if there is no sin, then there is no need for forgiveness, and sin is disobedience. When you forgive someone for sinning against you, that means you are forgiving them for disobedience. So once again we need to make a passing grade in the category of forgiveness for obedience sake.

The main reason, however, why we must make, not just a passing grade in forgiveness, but a perfect 100%, is because if you forgive all the sins that have ever been sinned against you, except for one, then the Lord will return the favor. He will forgive all your sins, except one. On the surface that sounds like a fairly good deal, and it is a pretty good deal. The problem is that it is not a good enough deal. You see sins are spots on your wedding garment: one sin is one spot on your wedding garment. A wedding garment must be spotless. In case you do not understand what the word spotless means; it means that you cannot have even one little spot on it! Being a Christian means we have all been invited to the wedding, by God himself, and we accepted God's invitation!

I think (Matthew 22:1-14) can explain it better than I can. 1 "And Jesus answered and spake unto them again by parable, and said, 2 The kingdom of heaven is like unto a certain king, which made a marriage for his son, 3 And sent forth his servants to call them that were bidden to the wedding: and they would not come. 4 Again, he sent forth other servants, saying Tell them which are bidden, Behold, I have prepared my dinner: my oxen and my fatlings are killed, and all things are ready; come unto the marriage. 5 But they made light of it, and went their ways, one to his farm, and another to his merchandise: 6 And the remnant took his servants, and entreated them spitefully, and slew them. 7 But when the king heard thereof, he was wroth: and he sent forth his armies, and destroyed those murderers, and burned up their city.

8 Then saith he to his servants, The wedding is ready, but they which were bidden were not worthy. 9 Go ye therefore into the highways, and as many as ye shall find, bid to the marriage. 10 So those servants went out into the highways, and gathered all as many as they found, both bad and good: and the wedding was furnished with guests. 11 And when the king came in to see the guests, he saw there a man which had not on a wedding garment: 12 And he saith unto him, Friend how camest thou in hither not having a wedding garment? And he was speechless. 13 Then said the king to the servants, Bind him hand and foot, and take him away, and cast him into outer darkness; there shall be weeping and gnashing of teeth. 14 For many are called, but few are chosen."

Also in (Matthew 6:14-15) it states, 14. "For if ye forgive men their trespasses, your heavenly Father will also forgive you: 15. But if ye forgive not men their trespasses, neither will your Father forgive your trespasses." So forgiveness is a powerful tool that you can use to keep anyone who sins against you from being condemned to the lake of fire, for whatever they did to you. Yes! As a Christian you have that kind of power. If you use this power as the Lord instructs you to, and use it every single time as the Lord instructs you to: then this same power will forgive you right on into the kingdom of heaven, every single time provided that you also pass the other three categories! This category alone has a power like no other, because if you get anything less than a perfect score, you will condemn yourself!

Let us say you inherited 10 million dollars. All you have to do to claim it is stand in one spot and catch a bus to go pick in up. If while you are waiting, I walk up to you, punch you, slap you, spit in your face and then walk away. What will you do? Walk away from the bus stop, catch me and get even, or stay, wait on the bus, catch it and receive your inheritance? Forgiveness is staying for your inheritance no matter what. People will refuse to accept 10 million dollars for whatever is left of their temporary life: even if they only have 6 months left to live. But will sell their guaranteed permanent life for 100,000 dollars. The worst part is God is the one who guarantees it! For some strange reason we place greater value on temporary life than we do permanent life!

Yes, you can forgive someone even if they are dead, but for your sake only, not for their sake. Their fate has already been decided. You can tell someone face-to-face that you forgive them or you can tell the Lord. Do not deceive your own self into thinking that you have forgiven someone, when in reality you have not. (Example) Because I have always feared the Lord, I would always forgive people for whatever they did to me. Sometimes it would take a while, but I always did it unless I waited too long and messed around and forgot to. So to be on the safe side, every now and then, I would tell the Lord when I said my prayers at night that I forgive anybody I forgot to forgive. But somewhere in my past I remember someone telling me, "You be sure to forgive them and let the good Lord get even with them."

So for many years, that was pretty much how I forgave people. Until one time my little brother, Ronnie, sinned against me, and I figured it to be a pretty serious sin before the Lord. So when I told the Lord in my prayers that I forgive Ronnie, I also told the good Lord that I want the whole thing to be on me. I didn't want him to do anything at all to Ronnie, no punishment or nothing. As a matter of fact let it be just like I gave it to him. Because he had taken something from me. Well to make a long story short, it was right then and there that the Holy Spirit pointed out to me, that I had finally learned how to forgive.

When you forgive someone, you do not have to trust them again. You do not have to like their company and you do not have to be happy towards them. If they took something from you, you don't have to let them have it unless they cannot afford to return it to you. Just because you have them to return your property does not mean you have failed to truly forgive them. But the Lord is even more pleased when you go ahead and allow them to keep it.

Remember, when you forgive someone, you also stop the hand of God from punishing them on your behalf. As much as the Lord may want to punish someone, he will honor the fact that you choose to forgive them. The Lord would not have given us this kind of power if he did not intend to honor it himself! This power is honored on earth and in heaven!

The fourth category we will be graded on is obedience. Obedience is a category in which none of us has done well. No one who knows the difference between right and wrong will score perfectly when it comes to obedience, with the exception of Christ himself. Your own personal obedience must start at some point, and it must show evidence of continuous improvement, and where it falls short, the other three categories will carry you through. This is why we must do well in the other three categories. The other three are not hard for us to do well in because whether you are aware of it or not, to do well in the other three categories is in fact the act of being obedient in three major areas.

Another thing you should be aware of is the fact that our obedience is taken into consideration from three different points of view. The first view is before we got saved. *The second view is after we got saved. There is a big difference between sins before you were saved, and sins after you got saved. Our sins that we commit after we get saved have a bigger price. The third point of view is after you come into the knowledge that there is a big difference between sin before salvation, and sin after salvation. The Lord has put it in my heart to let this be known because many of us who are saved did not know this. So if you did not know, well now you know!*

Chapter 20

Reality, Eternity & Illusion

I will start by saying that, to a four-year-old child, Santa Claus is a reality. You can explain to the child all you want concerning the fact that Santa Claus is a myth, but you will make very little progress, if any at all. At least not as long as the child is that young. As the child grows older, he or she will come to the knowledge that what they once viewed as reality was actually a distortion of reality itself.

In other words, it was an illusion. I would suppose that since I have made mention of both reality and illusion, it would only be fitting to also mention eternity.

Eternity does last forever but foreverness is nowhere near the full definition of eternity. As far as the concept of reaching a place in the universe where we will begin living forever is concerned, we are already there. We all have entered a place where we have begun living, and there is no hope at all for anyone of us who sincerely wishes to stop living. We can only shed flesh and continue on down or up the path we are already on.

The assertion that eternity is a place where there is no such thing as time is a myth. The world as we know it is nothing but a very small sample of the world we have heard about all our lives. A sample is an amount of something that is so small that it can only be used or experienced a fraction of the time that the whole product itself can be used or experienced. But the connection between the sample and the whole product is the assurance that elements or characteristics found in the sample of a product are indeed in the product itself.

Everything in the sample of life that we live in has to answer to time. Nothing can be done or undone without time. Whatever we learn, we must have enough time to learn it. Whatever we forget, we must have enough time to forget, if we ever forget it at all. God himself sat aside some of the stuff we call time in order to get him some rest after creating the world we live in. So to assume that the number one element in the sample does not exist in the product itself is an extremely incorrect assumption. By paying attention to what is in the sample, we know what is going to be in the product itself, only better and much-much more. We needn't worry ourselves with how much more, being that our imagination is satisfied with the good news that there will be much-much more of the things we love the most about the sample of life we have experienced so far.

Falling in love and time to enjoy having fallen in love. There are many reasons why we should want to leave this sample of life and enter into life itself, but if a young boy has ever fell in love with a young girl or young girl a boy, then that is reason enough to want to enter into Life the Product! In the world we live in a man doesn't even get enough time to taste what it is like to fall in love with a woman or woman a man. We do, however, get enough time to smell what it is like for a man to fall in love with a woman or woman a man. Even then we have to take an oath to stay together until this sample of life ends. In other words, get married.

In the world that awaits us, there will be no need to swear or take an oath that you will do this or do that, and to remain with the one you fall in love with is just one of the many things that you will not have to enter into an oath in order to experience. This is why Jesus said in (Luke 20:34-36) 34 "And Jesus answering said unto them, The children of this world marry, and are given in marriage: 35 But they which shall be accounted worthy to obtain that world, and the resurrection from the dead, neither marry, nor are given in marriage: 36 Neither can they die any more: for they are equal unto the angels; and are the children of God, being the children of the resurrection."

Consider this, in the world we now live in a person at the age of 21 has only begun to taste life. At that age they are well beyond believing Santa Claus is a reality. Because we as humans live forever, it means that although we now consider this world we live in now to be life, there will come a time in which we will look back at this period of our lives and know for sure that we were under the illusion that this was life. The reason I said before that we only get a chance to smell what life is like rather than taste what it is like, is because if you compare the amount of soup required in order for the taste buds to simply taste it to the amount required to only smell it, we will find that the amount required to only smell the soup is more than 100 times less. This why the sample of life that we live is considered more of a smell instead of a taste.

If you look at the numbers you can understand better what I am saying. Eternity is actually a time zone in which God and all angelic beings live in. In this time zone 1,000 earth years is the equivalent of one day. This is proved in 2nd Peter 3:8, "But, beloved, be not ignorant of this one thing, that one day is with the Lord as a thousand years, and a thousand years as one day" This is how long a day is in eternity. Further proof is in

Psalms 90:4, "For a thousand years in thy sight are but as yesterday when it is past... ... " This means that when 1,000 years have passed, the Lord calls that yesterday. 4&1/6 days of man's time= 1 second in eternity. 8&1/3 months of man's time= 1 minute in eternity. 41years&8months= 1 hour in eternity. 1,000 years of man's time= 1 day in eternity.

The earth has only existed a little over 12,000 years. It took 6,000 years to create, plus it has been in existence 4,000 years before Jesus was born and 2,015 years sense he has been gone. That equals only 12,015 years. It would take 360,000 of man's years by the Jewish calendar to equal only 1 year in eternity's time zone, and 365,000 by the modern day calendar. It would take 21 times 365,000 earth years in order for anyone of us to reach the age of 21 in eternity's time zone. At which point the Lord himself will say to us, "Children, you have only began to taste what it is like to fall in love with someone." If we live to be 83 years old, we have only lived 2 hours in the eyesight of the Lord! Now do you understand what I mean when I say that in this very small sample of life that we live we only have enough time to smell what it is like to fall in love with someone? The Lord lives in eternity and he calls it reality. We live on the earth and we call this reality. One is reality and one is the illusion that it is reality. You decide.

Earlier in this book I mention that I was caught up to heaven in a vision and that a whitish color horse having no rider came before me. Twelve years ago a man that I had never seen before in my life walked up to me and said to me that I had been touched by the finger of God, and that he had given me an unbelievable ministry. That is who was on the horse and this book is the ministry.

www.ingramcontent.com/pod-product-compliance
Lightning Source LLC
Chambersburg PA
CBHW060641150426
42811CB00078B/2236/J